REAL ESTATE MASTERY

REAL PROFITS
REAL STRATEGIES
REAL RESULTS

DAVID LEON

Contents

Disclaimer

The contents provided in this book belong to the copyright holder Real Estate Mastery Limited, and are intended ONLY for personal use, and are strictly not for copying, replication, printing, scanning or distribution. Any other use is strictly prohibited by copyright laws.

Whilst best endeavours have been made to ensure accuracy in all content of this book we do not guarantee any information, and disclaim all liability for any act or omission (including failure to act) in relation to content provided in this book. The information provided in this book is not intended to replace legal, accounting or any other professional service. We recommend that you contact specific experts when implementing the strategies provided in this book or any other property investing strategies.

Reproduction or translation of any part of this work without written permission from a director of Real Estate Mastery Limited is illegal.

Special Thanks

I am very lucky to have a great team of professionals behind all my business and investment endeavours. Without all of you I would not be able to do what I do.

Firstly, I want to thank my business partner in Real Estate Mastery, and numerous deals, Blake Montague. You are an inspiration to me and thousands of people around the world. Your easy-going and fun-loving personality is contagious. I look forward to many decades of working hard and playing even harder brother!

Thanks also to my team in Real Estate Mastery who work relentlessly to deliver the best property investing product in New Zealand and probably on the planet. Your passion to help others selflessly is just beautiful.

In addition, thanks to our office staff, who I love spending quality time with because you inspire me to deliver a better product to our customers.

My Ozzie brother, Ben Doyle – not only do we have the most epic times when we get together, but we push each other to do better in all aspects of life. You are awesome mate.

Most importantly thanks to my wife, Christina, and daughter, Sofia, who make me smile and feel accomplished in my life every time I look at them. I know I am very lucky to have you both. Chrissie, you have been there for us from day one, through good times and not so good ones; through all our learning and growing experiences; through all the tough and easy decisions; and not once has your love, loyalty and commitment to our relationship wavered. All my business decisions are made easier by knowing that even when I mess up, you will be there supporting me and letting me know that things will get better and that you believe in me and us. It is hard to put into words how much this means to me. Thank you seems like the biggest understatement. I will keep doing what I do to create even more amazing memories that we will cherish for a lifetime. Sofia, you are my world and seeing you grow up is the biggest of gifts I have ever received, I love you more than words could ever express.

Introduction

Whether the property market is going up, down or sideways you can still profit from property in NZ. We are extremely lucky to live in one of the most pro-property investor countries in the world. From taxation to tenancy laws, we are geared to be able to amass great wealth through smart property investing. When my seminar attendees, mates and business partners overseas learn about how good we have it here in NZ, they are always perplexed and even slightly incredulous about just how good it is in the land of the long white cloud. After letting the information sit for a short while they will always find a way to get involved in the market here if they are serious about their commitment to creating wealth through property investing.

Just in case you need to count your blessings when it comes to property investing in NZ, here is my top 10 of why we are so lucky to be investing in arguably the most beautiful country in the world:

Capital gains tax at 0%.

NO stamp duty – the UK has just raised stamp duty an extra 3% on all property investment purchases. This means you could be paying over 5% on stamp duty tax to purchase a property in the UK.

NO wealth tax.

Very little red tape in property transactions.

No gazumping! Sales and purchase agreements create simple and easy transactions eliminating vendors pulling out of contractual obligations if they just feel like it.

Pro-landlord tenancy laws (compared to other Western countries).

Simple and affordable company set up. Anyone with a few hundred dollars can set up their own company.

Virtually no corruption, we take this for granted and we never should. This is a big deal to a lot of the foreign clients that I work with.

Advanced and relatively straightforward banking system.

Fantastic yields and other property deal opportunities.

There is no excuse for not getting involved in this fantastic market and the only regret you will have is not to have already done so. The amount of foreign money we have seen coming into the country lately is a direct result of these fantastic opportunities we have in our backyard. We live in a very desirable "neighbourhood" on the planet and demand will only increase as transport becomes more efficient, easier and more affordable. We will become more accessible to the rest of the world as technology advances. Demand will therefore keep outstripping supply and creating more opportunities for further property price increases in the right areas. The future definitely looks great for educated investors in the land of the long white cloud.

The real question here is whether you are ready to take advantage of this opportunity. The main reason why people tell me they are not ready to pull the trigger and take action is because of a lack of education and knowledge. I assume that is the reason you are reading this book. There are different strategies that you can apply in today's market to maximise profits whilst minimising exposure and risks. This book covers quite a few of them but its content is useless unless you get off your "ass-ets" and start creating the right portfolio for you. There is no clear right or wrong in property investing, there is though what is right for you and what is not right for you. So before you start learning the "how to", make sure you first have an introspective journey into your own world where you will discover just how much you need to live the life of your dreams.

Do not get started until you discover this very important piece of the puzzle. Life is all about being happy, not being wealthy. Wealth definitely makes happiness come a bit easier, but accumulating wealth for the sake of it will only lead to dissatisfaction. I always ask my audiences to know and clearly understand what they really want in their lives so they can design the right plan with the right strategy mix for them and so they will know when to stop and "smell the roses".

This book will be your first mentor into the fascinating and ever-changing world of property investing. It will guide you through your initial steps into the unknown, hold your hand through your first deal and even enlighten you about a new way of closing a property transaction. Mentors are essential for any business owner or investor. Having someone to share your problems with and shed some light into the opportunities ahead will become the most valuable part of your business. Free advice could be the most expensive advice you ever get. Make sure your mentor is where you want to be and has enough knowledge, resources and contacts to assist you on your journey.

"Learn to enjoy the journey, not just the destination." One of my favourite personal quotes. Most people are so focused on getting there that they end up wishing away over 80% of their lives. The learning experiences, the people you will meet, the wins you will have are all worth just as much, if not more, than the end result. Learn to enjoy every single step and do your work as an investor with a sense of joy and happiness. Sounds corny but it is some of the best advice I ever got from one of my mentors, Kevin Green.

Market Condition Commentary

Today's market conditions are volatile. The huge and slightly crazy property price pump that we experienced in the early stages of the pandemic created a bubble that had to eventually pop. Besides this incredibly important factor there is one far bigger to consider: Money Printing (or qualitative easing as our corrupt politicians describe it to make you feel like they are not printing money out of thin air). Most western governments decided that it would be a good idea to increase money while they locked down countries and decimated their businesses (especially small and medium sized businesses) and economies. I obviously was a very strong and vocal opposer to these policies but unfortunately we now have to live with the consequences. We are experiencing high levels of inflation and we are trying to blame other world events for the fact that governments made a huge mistake. For example, 40% of all US Dollars were printed in 2020!!! Seriously, this is a fact. 40% of ALL US DOLLARS ever printed in history!!! INSANE!!!

Inflation has in turn artificially softened the property market which is heavily driven by cashflow and returns. Higher interest rates followed high inflation which then led to higher mortgages and rents but still lower cashflow. This lower cashflow created lower property prices.

To me it seems abundantly obvious that these interest rate hikes won't do much by themselves besides crippling our businesses which rely heavily in borrowed capital. These will in turn create a market crash followed by high unemployment. Yes, our downward market has literally just started.

The devaluation of local currencies will create a good paradigm for people holding assets. Let me explain. If your dollars can buy less things, then everything increases in price, (number of dollars to purchase) especially assets like property. Higher unemployment will also create a larger number of tenants which in turn will create higher rentals and yields therefore producing higher price increases to the rental property stock.

Let me explain further. If you have $100,000 in the the bank or saved under the mattress and you apply inflation to it then the value of your money goes down. Say 20% inflation means your $100,000 are now "worth" $80,000. If you invest those $100,000 in property you are effectively protecting yourself from inflation by buying an asset that is becoming more valuable because it is producing higher returns. That asset assuming 20% inflation will go up at least 20% (likely more because of all the other forces described previously) meaning that you are at least 40% better off holding properties than holding cash. That 40% also doesn't take into account that in a flat or downward market it is normal to get discounted property. 10-20% would be considered a reasonable discount meaning you are actually better off by over 50%!

In summary, the only real risk you have in this market is that YOU DO NOT INVEST and hold your devaluating cash waiting for a bargain. Cash is trash, cashflow is king and saving is expensive.

Preface

This is a no-nonsense book designed to give you the guts of effective and profitable property investing in NZ. In my experience most of the concepts covered can also be applied in the Australian and British markets with obvious tax and lending differences. It is not designed for a complete novice and it expects you to have some basic knowledge of terms and calculations commonly used in property investing. If you are a novice it will definitely take you longer to read it, but it will be the best learning experience you will ever have.

Part I of this book talks about the tools you will need to understand to be able to apply some of the strategies we will uncover in Part II. Part III is the how to use this information and making the most out of property investment section. I believe it is the most important part of this book since knowledge without action is just a waste of time.

You DO NOT have to apply all these strategies. There are quite a few of them that I personally do not pursue at all. I always compare having knowledge of these strategies with carrying a big toolbox when going into a renovation. You are very unlikely to use all the tools in your toolbox, but it is good to know they are there just in case a problem arises. You can therefore use this book as a reference resource when you have questions or need ideas on how to structure a deal so that it comes together as a win-win.

Once again, this book is specifically written and designed for the NZ market although people in other Western countries may find it useful nonetheless if they don't pay close attention to the systemic steps of each transaction which will differ slightly in each jurisdiction. Obviously tax laws do change from time to time in NZ and even though I have used my best endeavours to produce information that is accurate on today's market, I still advise you to take legal, financial or any other professional advice before making any investment decisions. This book is not designed to replace any professional advice or to give you personalised investment advice, it is all about educating you on the strategies that work in today's market conditions.

Enjoy this "how to" property investment strategy book and make sure you contact us if we can be of further service

.

Part I - Tools

Being prepared may determine whether you get or lose a fantastic and very profitable property deal. The more prepared investors with the biggest property strategy "toolkit" will get more and better deals than average, uneducated investors. Having your funding ready and mastering the usage of the standard Auckland Law Society's sales and purchase agreement are the most powerful elements of this toolkit. Without these elements there is no point in looking at actual property investment strategies.

I. Finance Your Portfolio Right

There are many different types of lenders from which to source the finance you need both to buy a property, and to fund the renovations you may require. These include banks, building societies, venture capitalists, credit unions, private capital, peer-to-peer lending and finance companies among others.

It can be a somewhat time-consuming task to find finance that works for you, so be prepared to clock up a few hours. That is where having a good broker on your side could be invaluable in saving you money, headaches and time.

When you are starting out, your personal income will be heavily taken into account in your ability to service the debt (serviceability). This can really help if you are buying a property that is under-performing rent-wise, as your income can be used to make up the difference. However, once you have a few properties under your belt, your income will not weigh so heavily into this equation, so you will need to have your properties paying for themselves if you are buying to hold and if you plan to acquire a significant portfolio. Do take into consideration that banks do not take 100% of your rental as income, usually they will take anything from 65-75% of the rental as realistic income in their serviceability calculations. If you plan on selling quickly you will need to convince the bank that you can make the repayments until you sell the property for a profit and pay back the loan. This is definitely not an easy task in today's market.

If you need to boost your income so that banks will be more likely to lend you money, you could always sell one of your other properties. The profit you make may be accounted for as part of your income for that year and you may look much healthier from a lender's perspective. Your new higher income will indicate to them that you are indeed capable of making the loan repayments. Note that some banks may not qualify this income as "servicing income".

Here are my top 6 tips to increase serviceability:

1. Maintaining a good credit score: Your credit score is a measure of your creditworthiness, which is the likelihood that you'll repay a loan. A good credit score shows banks that you're a responsible borrower, and can help improve your chances of getting approved for a loan. To maintain a good credit score, make sure you pay your bills on time, keep your credit card balances low, and avoid applying for too much credit in a short period of time.

2. Staying organized: Keeping accurate records of your income, expenses, and assets can help you track your financial situation, identify areas for improvement, and demonstrate your financial stability to a lender. When applying for a loan, you'll need to provide financial

documentation, such as proof of income, bank statements, and tax returns, so it's important to have these records ready and up-to-date.

3. Understanding your financial needs: Knowing how much money you need and why you need it will help you communicate your needs to the bank effectively and make it easier for the bank to assess your loan application. It can also help you determine if a loan is the best solution for your financial situation, or if there are other options available, such as reducing expenses or finding ways to increase your income.

4. Building a relationship with your bank: Building a good relationship with your bank can help you receive better customer service, get more favorable loan terms, and have a better overall experience. This can include opening a savings or checking account, using their services regularly, and being proactive about communicating with the bank when you need help or have questions.

5. Shop around: Compare loan offers from different banks to find the best rates and terms. Banks offer a range of loans, from personal loans to mortgages, so it's important to understand what's available and compare offers from different lenders. By shopping around, you can find the loan that best meets your needs and saves you the most money.

6. Being proactive: Keep in touch with your bank or broker, especially if your financial situation changes, so that you can stay on top of any updates or changes in your loan terms. For example, if your income changes, you may need to adjust the amount you can afford to repay each month, or if you're having difficulty making your payments, you may need to work with the bank to find a solution. By being proactive, you can keep your loan in good standing and improve your chances of getting approved for future loans.

Organise your personal finances

It is important to get your personal finances in order first before you race off to the bank to borrow millions or at least hundreds of thousands of dollars. Once you get your personal finances under control you can start making offers. Talk to a professional advisor so that they can help you get in control of your financials in order to maximise your potential today and for the future.

Here are my top 8 tips to organise your personal finances:

1. Create a budget: Start by creating a budget to track your income and expenses and understand where your money is going. This can help you identify areas where you can cut back on spending and prioritize your spending.

2. Automate your finances: Automating your finances can help you keep on top of your bills and reduce the risk of missed payments, which can harm your credit score. Consider setting up automatic bill payments and direct deposit of your paychecks.

3. Track your spending: Keep track of your spending by using a budgeting app, spreadsheet, or pen and paper. This can help you identify areas where you may be overspending and make adjustments to your budget as needed.

4. Set financial goals: Setting financial goals, such as saving for a down payment on a house, paying off debt, or building an emergency fund, can help you focus your efforts and keep you motivated.

5. Pay off debt: High levels of debt can limit your financial flexibility and increase your risk of financial stress. Consider creating a plan to pay off your debt, starting with high-interest debt first.

6. Save for the future: Building a solid emergency fund and saving for retirement can help you protect yourself against unexpected expenses and ensure a secure financial future.

7. Protect your assets: Protect your assets by getting insurance coverage for your health, home, car, and other valuable items. This can help you stay financially secure if the unexpected occurs.

8. Seek professional help: If you need help with your finances, consider seeking professional advice from a financial advisor, accountant, or other financial professional. They can help you understand your financial situation, create a budget, and develop a plan to achieve your financial goals.

Your financial information

You need to know your net worth – you may be surprised how many people don't! To do this, calculate the net value of your assets minus your debt and you will have your net worth. For example if you own your own home worth $900,000, a rental worth $400,000 with a total mortgage of $750,000 and unencumbered shares and other assets like cars worth $100,000 and savings of $50,000 you would be worth: 900,000+400,000+100,000+50,000-750,000= $700,000.

You should also calculate your cash flow position. Work out exactly what your income and expenses are, as well as your assets and liabilities, as this is information your lender will need. Financiers will be much more impressed, and therefore more willing to lend you money if you can present this information in an orderly fashion. If you are vague and disorganised a lender will most likely be less than keen to give you large amounts of money. A broker can assist you to present this information in the best light possible.

Prepare budgets

You will also need to prepare budgets to work out the money you need for the purchase of the property as well as any planned renovations.

Keep your finances as simple as you possibly can – all sorts of blunders can happen when things get overly complicated. At the very least make sure you understand all your financing arrangements fully.

Budgeting is simply figuring out how you want to divvy up your dough. By creating a plan for your income and expenses, you can keep your spending in check, track your progress, and make changes to reach your financial goals.

First things first, track your income and expenses for a month. This will give you a good idea of where your money is going and what you can cut back on. Next, group your expenses into categories like housing, transportation, food, and entertainment. This will help you see how much you're spending in each area and where you can save some cash.

Tools

Now it's time to create your budget. Decide how much you want to spend in each category and stick to it. Make sure your expenses don't exceed your income and adjust your budget if necessary.

Setting financial goals is also important, so don't forget to include them in your budget. For example, if you want to save for a down payment on a house, set aside some cash each month. If you have high-interest debt, make a plan to pay it off and put money towards it each month.

Remember, being flexible is key. Life changes and so should your budget. If your income goes up, think about putting more towards savings or allowing yourself to spend a little extra in areas you've been cutting back on.

Lastly, track your progress and regularly review your budget and expenses to make sure you're on track. Using a budgeting app or spreadsheet can help you stay organized.

In short, budgeting is a must-do if you want to take control of your finances and reach your financial goals. By tracking your income and expenses, creating a budget, setting goals, and being flexible, you'll be well on your way to financial stability.

Know your credit rating

You need to know what your credit rating is before you apply for finance. There are currently three companies in NZ that store your credit file and you need to check all three since the information kept in all three is different. Here are the three companies with their respective websites:

Centrix: www.centrix.co.nz/

Dun & Bradstreet: www.checkyourcredit.co.nz/

Veda Advantage: http://mycreditfile.co.nz/

It's free to get a copy of your credit record, but if you want the information promptly you will need to pay for it.

Your credit file will show how many times you have applied for finance and every time you have defaulted. It will not say whether the finance you applied for was approved or declined, or whether you accepted it or not. If you have applied for finance frequently, as is necessary when you are investing in property, your lender may be a little concerned, so it pays to know in advance so you can explain yourself!

Tools

Improving your credit "worthiness"

If you need to improve your credit rating because it is ugly enough to cause potential lenders to roll around on the floor with laughter at your request for finance, take heart – there are things you can do.

•   Paying all your bills on time is a great way to start on the road to a good credit rating.

•   Get a steady job – if you are unemployed, or just work sporadically, the lenders will look less favourably on you.

•   Stay at the same address – moving house every few months is not a good sign as far as lenders go.

•   Apply for several credit cards, use them and make the payments every month. This will show that you are indeed responsible, especially if you keep the amount you owe on the cards less than half the available credit. If you have a proven history of paying back money you owe on time, it will definitely work in your favour. Even if you are a person who pays bills, has a steady job and always lives within their means, if you have never borrowed money and paid it back before, your credit rating will not be as healthy as someone who has. It pays to get a few credit cards!

Preparing to see the lender

Be very well prepared when you go to see a lender. You will need all the information you have about the property you are planning to purchase, as well as details about your own personal financial situation. Once again I recommend new investors do not visit lenders directly and employ the services of a good mortgage broker.

Lenders can be a little wary of properties that need work, especially the more run-down ones. They will, however, be impressed by thorough research, especially if it backs up your claims that the property will make a profit and their money will be safe. You need to show them also that you are in a position to make the loan payments.

Present all this information in a professional manner – that does not mean scribbled on the back of a paper napkin! If you just waltz in without documenting what you are planning to do to the property and how this will increase its value or rental income, the bank may baulk at the idea of you buying something that is so obviously in desperate need of renovation work. You need to make your lender feel confident about lending you money – or they are unlikely to give you a dollar.

Getting finance

A. Get pre-approval for finance

Aim to get pre-approval for finance as soon as possible, and definitely before you start looking for properties. Once you have your finance pre-approved by your lender, you can go and look for a property. Just remember, pre-approval does not guarantee you will get the money – there may be something about the property the bank doesn't like which will mean your loan may not be approved.

B. Work out all the fees

To prevent any nasty surprises, get the fees for the loan in writing. Also remember that fees are negotiable. Almost every fee that any lender demands can be negotiated. You don't just have to just accept them! Make sure you never pay fees up front before a loan is approved. Always ask for more than you expect to get, you may be surprised with what you end up getting.

C. Check the loan's clauses

You must check them because different loan agreements will have different clauses, and you need to do some research to find out what will work best for you. Quite often you will find that a loan with low or no entry fees will not have features that are important to you, so check it out. (And remember my previous point that fees are negotiable!)

Many lenders will offer better deals to people who will be living in the property they want to borrow money for. This is one advantage of using the live-in-while-you-renovate strategy. Do not lie in your mortgage application; mortgage fraud is a criminal offence and this means you could go to jail – not just be declined or even fined for it.

D. Shop around for the best interest rates

Always shop around for interest rates. It is a good idea to compare the interest rates various lenders are offering, so you know what is available, and so you can negotiate with a lender you like (see our point below). Interest rates can also differ between different branches of the same bank, so it pays to do your research. You can find this information on the Internet, or if you are using a mortgage broker they will be able to compare rates for you.

Believe it or not, interest rates are negotiable too. Do your research so you know what the other lenders are offering and use this information to negotiate. The lender may disguise a reduction in the interest rate as a decrease in, or waiver of fees, but over the term of the loan you will have to pay less so it equates to a lower interest rate.

E. State your intentions, even if they change later...

State your position at the time when applying for finance – and know you can change your mind later. For example, you can say when you apply for the loan that you are going to rent the property out so that the rental income will be taken into account with regard to your ability to service the loan. If you happen to change your mind after you have received the money and decide to sell the property after renovating, it is no skin off the lender's nose, as long as you make the required payments until you sell and discharge the loan.

Remember, however, not to intentionally pull the wool over your lender's eyes, as you will be caught out (especially if you can't make payments) and your credit rating will be – to put it bluntly – screwed.

F. Avoid the one-bank trap

A bank manager's goal is to keep you as a valued customer and to stop you from going to other banks. However, it is much easier to borrow $3 million from five banks than it is from one, so don't be sucked in by their overtures. If you stay with one bank all your collateral property will be with them. You will find yourself stuck and unable to buy more property when they have lent you the maximum amount they are comfortable with.

If you are with a bank but have reached your maximum borrowing limit with them, ask if they will make more loans available to you if you discharge some of the debt to other lenders. Obviously a good broker will ensure your lending strategy is properly set up from day one and you will not fall for the one-bank trap.

Loan strategies

A. Have loans maturing at different times

Have the loans for different properties maturing at different times, so that you spread your risk over time. If they all mature at once, and it just happens to be a time when the interest rates are experiencing a temporary high, you could be in for a bit of strife!

B. Personal guarantees for loans

All loans will require some sort of personal guarantee. However, you can limit this to the debt level, rather than an unlimited level. It is best not to request this when applying for the loan, though, as your lender may have some resistance to the idea. You don't want them to think that perhaps they shouldn't be lending you the money in the first place. Instead, your lawyer can approach the bank once the documents have been received. The bank will be much more agreeable to limiting the guarantee to the loan amount if it is approached from a legal perspective.

C. Avoid using equity in one property as security for another

Avoid using equity in one property as security over another. This is a trap many people fall into. Rather than using the equity in one property as security over another, you are better to take the equity out as cash and put that into the next property. If you don't, you can find yourself getting into all sorts of difficulties and restricting your options, because when you sell one property, the profit will have to be used to reduce the debt of the other one.

D. Use revolving credit

Take advantage of revolving-credit facilities – otherwise known as a line-of-credit loan. This means that you can access any extra equity whenever you like, so you can fund your next purchase. For example, if you have a property worth $400,000 and you are able to borrow up to 80%, the amount available to you will be $320,000. If you only use $200,000 of this for your mortgage, you have the extra $120,000 to play with. If you then put this on a revolving line of credit you can use it to fund your next property purchase(s).

The option of vendor finance

Vendor financing is when the seller of a product or service is the one providing the financing. It's a pretty sweet deal for small biz owners or individuals who might not have the best options with traditional financing like a bank loan.

The best part about vendor financing is that you get to call the shots on the terms of the loan. You can negotiate the interest rate, payment schedule, and all that jazz to make sure it works for you and your cash flow.

Getting vendor financing can also be a faster process compared to other forms of financing. If the vendor is on board, it can be smooth sailing and you could get the green light pretty quickly. Just keep in mind that the vendor will usually want a big down payment, so make sure you have enough saved up before jumping in.

In some rare cases, you might even be able to get 100% financing from the vendor. But, you'll probably have to give up some of your profits to make it happen. Still, this could be a good option if you're starting from scratch or need to buy a big item and don't have the dough.

In short, vendor financing is a solid choice for those who want more control over their loan and want a flexible financing solution. Just make sure you have a motivated vendor and enough cash saved up for a big down payment.

So you need 100% funding, what are your options?

In the event that you do not have enough money for a deposit and vendor financing is not going to work, you will need 100% financing to be able to buy a property. There are quite a few options available to you if you need to do this – just be creative! If the option you do choose has a high interest rate attached to it, make sure you factor this into your costings and repay the loan as fast as possible.

If the bank will not loan you 100%, you could consider:

Selling something, such as your car, to create the required additional funds.

Credit cards

Credit cards are also a possibility especially for small deposits or renovations. You may use your credit card not to buy a house, but for the deposit. Be very sure that you can make the monthly payments before you decide on this course of action. Low balance transfer credit card opportunities make this option very favourable to the astute investor. I personally used this strategy to get started using none of my own money.

C. Private equity investors

A private investor could be another source of finance if you can't persuade the bank that you are a low risk profile for them. A private investor may even just lend you enough for a deposit, which may be all you need. Also friends and family, if they cannot lend you the hard cash, may be willing to offer you a guarantee or provide collateral so you are able to get a loan. They may also be generous enough to give you the money for your deposit or, in exceptional circumstances, the money for the whole property. Speak nicely to them!

D. Partnerships and joint ventures

Partnerships and joint venture partnerships (which are similar but different) are another way of getting finance if the bank is not interested in you on your own. Either one can provide a means of completing a project that you couldn't do by yourself. Partnerships generally have unlimited risk for the partners, whereas in joint ventures the risk can be restricted. In a partnership each partner needs to find their own finance, but in a joint venture financing can be arranged together.

You will need to set up the structure and agreements for either type of partnership very carefully, detailing who is responsible for what, how the profit will be divided and what to do if one partner is not pulling their weight or wants out. Use a lawyer to draw up the agreement and to give you advice on which sort of partnership will suit your needs, and the needs of your partner(s), best.

Partnerships and joint ventures not only provide the extra finance you may need, they are also a great way for people of like minds but different skills to work together. For example, you could provide the renovations skill and the partner the money. A partnership is also an excellent way to go if your partner is more experienced than you, because they will be able to guide you through the process and you will learn a huge amount while gaining valuable experience. Use partners a single project at a time – it is unlikely that you will want to be joined at the hip for life!

E. Peer-to-peer lending

This is a very new strategy that some of our clients are currently using to bridge the money requirement needed to invest in property. I believe this strategy exceeds the scope of this book but I have put together a comprehensive report about peer-to-peer (otherwise known as social) lending in NZ that is available upon request once you join our program.

Refinancing

Remember, you will be able to refinance your loan every time you get a new valuation for properties you are holding on to – as long as it is higher than the last one! You should get your first new valuation done after you have completed your renovations. If your original loan was for 80% of the property's value, each time you revalue you should be able to refinance up to 80% of the new improved value. Then you can use this extra money to fund more properties – and the empire building will have begun!

If you have financed your property other than through a normal lending institution (e.g. partnership, very kind and trusting father, private mortgage) and you want to hold on to it rather than sell, you should be able to refinance on the new valuation (especially if the rent has increased to cover the outgoings) from a conventional lender so your cash flow does not suffer.

Recycle your deposit

Work to recycle your deposit as quickly as possible. (By recycling we mean that the increase in the value of a property will allow you to refinance and use the new equity as a deposit for the next property.) The fastest way we know of to recycle your deposit is to buy under market value by being a market expert followed by adding value to a property with cosmetic renovations. Cosmetic renovations is by far the quickest and easiest, and may allow you to get your deposit back out in a month or so – which by property standards is pretty darn fast work! Make sure you take before and after photos to show the bank so they will be impressed and keen to refinance the property for you to keep building your wealth. If the bank is not happy with your work make sure you talk to other banks who will be more forthcoming with their funds. This is a very competitive market and sometimes a bank saying no only means they do not have the liquidity to lend rather than you or your property not being loan worthy.

Beware of thinking that you are adding value through renovations when you are really not doing anything of the sort. This is where doing thorough research before you launch full blast into a project will really pay off. For example, you may think that adding a few rooms and turning a house into a rent-by-the-room property is an excellent idea because you will be able to get more rent. If you haven't done your research properly, what you won't know is that the bank will most likely see this as student accommodation and they will not consider that you have added value from a lending point of view. What this means is that you won't be able to top up your mortgage to fund the next project because they won't give you any more money. Research is essential!

Mortgage brokers

Good leverage of your time

Use a mortgage broker unless you are experienced at finding finance, or you enjoy the challenge. It can be a complicated and tiring process finding the funds you require, and the knock-backs can be disheartening. A mortgage broker can take all this stress away from you, as it is their job to find the finance for you. They work for you, not the bank. They know where to look and have great bargaining power with the banks. You can tell a mortgage broker everything about your situation and they will know how much to tell lenders and, more importantly, when.

All this can make a huge difference to your success rate and goes a long way to reducing your stress levels. Finding finance can be incredibly time consuming, so a mortgage broker can be a very good leverage of your time.

Finding a broker

If you are going to use a mortgage broker, they will need to be good at what they do. You will want to find one who is an investor or deals mainly with investors. Often, but not always, you will find that small to medium-sized companies are better than one-man-bands or huge firms. Find out how they evaluate loans and if they have relationships with all the major lenders.

One of the best ways to find a good broker is to ask successful investors for referrals. You don't have to stick to just one mortgage broker and you are not obliged to accept loans they may find for you if you don't think it's a good deal. Don't be coerced into signing an agreement with them that states otherwise.

We highly recommend finding a quality mortgage broker who will work very closely with you and who understands property investment. Make sure you "click" with your mortgage broker, they are one of the most important people in your team.

Having a great mortgage broker in your team can make you a lot of money so treat them well if they do a good job. A good way of judging whether a mortgage broker will be good for you is if when you call them, you can talk to them at least 80% of the time. A good broker will let you know about the best products in the market and will offer you advice on the possibilities of restructuring your portfolio borrowings. A good connection is necessary with this member of your team – a point that we cannot stress enough.

Summary

You need to be prepared before you go and see your mortgage broker or your preferred lender. Have everything in order so that they can't say no to you. There are different components that you need to sort out in your personal finances before you apply for a loan, start taking care of them today.

Once you meet with your mortgage broker or your lender remember that all terms are negotiable, and that you should get the mortgage that fits your strategy.

There are different strategies you can use to obtain a high level of finance, leverage is important for a healthy portfolio.

Mortgage brokers can save you a lot of time and money through their contacts and knowledge of the industry. They will become a very important part of your power team.

(II)   Sales & Purchase Agreements and Clauses

Mastering sales and purchase agreements is a must for any successful property investor. You should be familiar with all the existing clauses in the standard sales and purchase agreement so you know your rights and responsibilities when things go wrong (as they tend to do every so often). Not only do you need to be familiar with the template, but also with the extra clauses you can insert to negotiate further terms before and after the agreement becoming unconditional. As a client, you will be provided with the clauses we have used for our property transactions. For the purposes of this book I will cover the most useful ones. Please do obtain legal advice before signing or entering any legal agreement. Remember this information is not to replace any legal or other professional advice.

Due diligence

This is the most common and unspecific clause used by property investors as a get-away clause from any deal they are uncertain about.

This agreement is conditional on the purchaser being satisfied in all respects and entirely at the purchaser's own discretion with the outcome of the purchaser's due diligence investigation into all aspects of the property and its suitability for the purchaser. If such approval has not been given in writing within x working days of the signing of this agreement by both parties, this agreement shall be null and void and all moneys under it shall be refunded in full and neither party shall have any claim against the other. This clause is inserted for the sole benefit of the purchaser and the vendor shall not be entitled to enquire into the purchaser's exercise of discretion under this clause.

Vendor's acceptance

I use this clause to add pressure to the vendor selling a property. The vendor will have the added pressure of knowing that the sale will fall through should the agreement not be accepted by the agreed time and date.

This offer will be deemed not to have been accepted and to have been withdrawn unless written notification of the vendor's acceptance of the offer is communicated to the vendor or the vendor's lawyer or to the estate agency acting on the sale (if any) by 5pm on _____.

Specialists' reports

These are great alternatives to the good old boring due diligence which plenty of agents and vendors do not like.

Tools

Builder's report

This agreement is conditional on the purchaser being satisfied in all respects with a building inspection report to be obtained by the purchaser for the property. This condition is to be satisfied within x working days of the date of this agreement.

Subject to engineer's report

This agreement is conditional on the purchaser being satisfied in all respects with an engineer's report to be obtained by the purchaser for the property. This condition is to be satisfied within x working days of the date of this agreement.

Local authority reports/enquiries

This agreement is conditional on the purchaser being satisfied in all respects with any reports the purchaser may wish to obtain from the local authority concerning the property and with any enquiries the purchaser may wish to make with the local authority. This condition is to be satisfied within x working days of the date of this agreement.

Conditional on sale of purchaser's property

Very common and useful if you need the money from another property sale to settle a new property purchase.

This agreement is conditional on the purchaser obtaining an unconditional sale contract for the purchaser's property situated at _____on such terms as are acceptable to the purchaser by 5pm on _____. This condition is inserted for the sole benefit of the purchaser. In this clause the term "unconditional" means unconditional in all respects including waiver/expiry of title requisition rights.

Access clauses

Gaining access in your due diligence or in the unconditional period can make you a lot of money and save you a lot of problems. Here are the most common ones:

Access to property on notice

On this agreement becoming unconditional the vendor will allow the purchaser reasonable access to the property (hours of access first to be approved by the vendor) to enable the purchaser to carry out cosmetic improvements to the property (excluding building works and structural works) and also for the purpose of showing the property to prospective tenants. All works are to be first approved by the vendor whose approval will not be unreasonably refused. The purchaser will ensure that no disruption or disturbance is caused to any tenants or occupiers of neighbouring properties.

Access for inspection

On this agreement becoming unconditional, the vendor will allow the purchaser access to the property to enable the purchaser's consultants and advisors to carry out inspections and tests as required.

Access for site inspections

On this agreement becoming unconditional, the vendor will allow the purchaser reasonable access to the property to enable the purchaser's consultants and advisors to carry out assessments and tests. This may include soil tests provided that the purchaser causes no damage to the property.

Access for quotations

Upon execution of the agreement by both parties, the vendor will allow the purchaser access to the property to enable the purchaser to obtain quotations for property renovations/additions.

Access for improvements and tenanting

On this agreement becoming unconditional, the vendor will allow the purchaser access to the property in order to carry out cosmetic improvements and/or to show the property to prospective tenants.

Cash-out clause

When you are trying to sell a property and the prospective purchaser gives you a contract with a long due diligence period, make sure you use this clause to "keep your options open."

If before this agreement becomes unconditional in all respects, the vendor obtains another offer on terms acceptable to the vendor, the vendor may deliver to the purchaser or the purchaser's solicitor notice in writing requiring the purchaser to confirm this agreement as being unconditional. The purchaser shall have until 4 p.m. on the working day after delivery of such notice to advise the vendor by delivery of notice in writing to the vendor or the vendor's solicitor that this agreement is unconditional, otherwise this agreement shall terminate.

Summary

Understanding the standard sales and purchase agreement and the additional clauses you can use is extremely important to be able to structure deals like a professional does. The more you use them the more proficient you will become at it. Make sure you take legal advice when necessary and that you use them to create win-win solutions to complete the deal.

(III)   Delayed Settlements

This clause is very important and could make you a lot of money if applied properly so I believe that it deserves its own separate section. The delayed settlement tool can be used to achieve several outcomes. It can definitely be used to achieve a no-money-down deal through a contemporaneous settlement. It can also be used to add value to a property while saving money on mortgage payments and maximising cash flow.

The way it works is very simple. In your sales and purchase agreement you can add the following clause as seen in section II:

Conditional on access and improvements:

The vendor agrees to provide the purchaser (and or its invitees) access to the property as many times as necessary in order to carry out a due diligence investigation.

Upon this agreement becoming unconditional, the purchaser may do all things necessary in order to carry out cosmetic improvements and/or secure a tenant/buyer.

You will also need to make the "possession date" as late as possible (delayed). You will display the date of possession or settlement on the first page of your sales and purchase agreement. The more work the property needs, the longer this period should be. At the end of the day, you will want to get as much as you can and the vendor will try to reduce it as much as he/she can, so you will just have to reach a compromise that suits both parties.

If the vendor agrees to your sales and purchase agreement, you will have access to the property from the time your agreement becomes unconditional. This will give you the opportunity to fix it up and show prospective buyers and/or tenants around.

Now is when the possibilities really start appearing with this strategy.

If you renovate the property you could get a valuation after you finish the repairs and before you settle on the property and the lender will be willing to lend you a mortgage based on the valuation price. On a normal deal they will only lend based on the valuation price or the purchase price, whichever is the smallest. They will be prepared to lend you based on valuation price because they know that you can get extra equity by repairing and improving a property. This lending could make your deal a no-money-down deal or very close to it.

You could also have enough time to find a tenant if you wanted to hold the property and rent it out. The advantage in this situation is that you will not have any vacancy periods when you buy the deal as most inexperienced investors do.

Instead of finding a tenant you could also find a buyer and then go into a contemporaneous settlement. Making it once again a no-money-down deal. A contemporaneous settlement is explained in part III of this book.

As you can see, this strategy has several advantages and can be used to produce very profitable outcomes. The great bonus with it is that it is very simple to apply. Only a couple of clauses in the sales and purchase agreement and you will be laughing all the way to the bank.

Summary

If you add an access clause to your sales and purchase agreement you will open up several possibilities to make a hefty amount of money through property renovations while minimising your risk and cash output. You can create contemporaneous settlements, renovate the property, get tenants and much more before you even settle! Negotiate a win-win outcome with the vendor and use these clauses effectively to create wealth where others just see problems.

(IV)   Tools for Sourcing Great Deals

A. Door knocking

It is amazing how many great deals we have found using this simple tool. Every time we buy or even get close to buying a property we knock on all the neighbours' doors and we introduce ourselves as property investors. We find that people attending our events had never apply this tool, and they miss out on great opportunities.

Private deals can be very profitable for investors, but you must understand and be an expert in your area so you can truly evaluate market value and make a reasonable offer. This is a skill that is basically impossible to explain in a book, but I will do my best to decipher it. Full immersion in a local area will make you very familiar with pricing on properties. Every street has its quirks and problems and you must know all of them to make really good informed decisions and avoid buying a lemon. The key here is full immersion. Market conditions in specific areas change considerably in short periods of time and you must keep up to date with the area so as to ascertain true market value.

Make sure you have business cards and/or brochures ready when you door knock. Most times a "No" really means "Not right now" and they could come back to you a few days or months down the line telling you they are ready to sell then.

I want to leave you with my top 5 tips for door knocking:

1. Preparation is key: Before you go door knocking, research the area and get to know the type of properties and potential sellers you're likely to encounter. This will help you tailor your pitch and increase your chances of success.

2. Make a strong first impression: Your appearance, demeanor, and approach can make all the difference when it comes to door knocking. Dress professionally, be friendly, and be confident in your pitch.

3. Be clear about your offer: When you're speaking with potential sellers, make sure to clearly explain what you're offering and why it's a good deal for them. Be prepared to answer any questions they may have and have any relevant materials ready to show them.

4. Follow up promptly: If a potential seller expresses interest, follow up with them promptly to keep the momentum going. This could mean sending them additional information, setting up a meeting, or just giving them a call to touch base.

5. Be persistent: Door knocking can be a time-consuming and often challenging process, but it can also be incredibly rewarding. Be persistent, stay positive, and keep trying even if you face rejection. With time and practice, you'll improve your skills and increase your chances of finding great property deals.

B. Classified ads

A much underused tool for finding these deals is the classified ad. You have several ways to benefit from this fantastic and easy-to-use tool that we all have easy and affordable access to.

The first step to take when using this technique is to find out which newspapers, magazines, internet sites people view when they are trying to purchase or rent a property. Once you know which ones are the most popular for the area you are targeting, then you can start this process.

I like to check if the market is ready for my strategy by placing ads before I purchase the property. By this time I already have an idea of which type of property is more sought after, but I like to double check by using the ad strategy. I will write ads that will look something like these ones depending on whether my strategy is to buy and sell or buy to let:

Renting

"Opportunity! 3 bedroom house available to rent in x area at only $x. Call Mary at 367 8251."

Buying

"Need to sell ASAP! 3 bedroom house for sale in x area at only $x. Must see. Call Susan at 215 7246."

Or

"Selling due to sickness, I am sick of living in this property! 3 bedroom house in x area at $x, call Melissa at 962 7220."

I always have female names on the ads because they are less intimidating for most people to call and talk to. You will receive more calls when you use a female name. If you are a male just answer the phone politely and explain to them that Mary is not available but you could help them.

At this stage I am only trying to check if there is demand for my properties by counting the number of phone calls I receive per ad placed and the level of interest from the people I speak to. Always specify the type of property, area and price when you are doing this exercise. Remember that you are assessing the market. Besides assessing the market you are also building a database of possible purchasers or tenants. When people call you to ask for "your" property you will tell them:

"I am so sorry! We just sold/rented that property, but we will be getting another one shortly in the area, so if I take down your name and number you will be the first one to know."

Now you have a possible customer and a clearer evaluation of the area that you are thinking of investing in. Now you are ready to place your second classified ad, the one that you will be getting good deals with:

"Private investor looking to buy 3 bedroom houses in the x area. Will pay cash. Call Christina at 210 5443."

Or

"Looking to purchase a 3 bedroom house in the x area. Cash available, call Jessica at 649 4289."

Both ads give very good results; the only difference between them is that the second one is a bit less aggressive because you will be seen as a first-time buyer. Decide on one or the other, depending on which option is less common on the advertising platform you choose. I personally like the second one better, but the first one has given me lots of very useful contacts too.

Identifying motivated sellers

After placing these ads you will then start receiving phone calls and the first question you need to ask is this one:

"Why are you selling the property?"

You ask this question to identify motivated sellers. You will be able to tell whether they are serious about selling so you can buy under market value. I want to clarify one concept before I go any further, please read carefully. I am not trying to rip anyone off! I do not mind leaving something on the table for the other party involved in the deal. If you feel that you keep ripping people off when you buy and sell property, you will not be in this business for long. You will provide people a service by not charging them any agency fees, not making them sign contracts and not having time wasters visiting their property. Besides that, you can also be flexible in terms of timing and that is worth quite a bit too. You can move in quickly, or wait until they are ready to move out. All these factors combined make up for the discount on the market price that you will be willing to pay. You are running a business and as long as it meets your buying rules you should buy and not worry about how much or little you leave on the table for the other party.

Get to know as much as you can about the seller because this way you will be able to offer them several alternatives to the sale of their property. This concept will become clearer when you read the next few strategies that will fit one type of seller or another. Ask about their time frames, ask about what they are expecting, ask about what they know about the buy-sell process and offer them some advice and help. You want them to like you, and there are simple techniques you can use to have a better chance of establishing the rapport you will need. Try to imitate their tonality of voice and their cadence of speech. Don't worry about being obvious about it, you will not be. People like people who are like themselves. We work these strategies in detail in our practical, on-the-ground, one-on-one mentoring programme.

Of all the phone calls you get, only a small percentage will be good leads. You have to identify these ones quickly and view them ASAP. Remember "the quick and the dead". The more you get used to receiving these phone calls, the better you will become at getting information and being able to sort them out.

Tools

C. Building relationships

I left the best and most important one for last. People underestimate the importance of creating long-lasting relationships with people in the industry that will feed you a constant number of deals regularly. I am not just talking about real estate agents but about any and every person that has access to property deals before they hit the market. These people include but are not limited to: property managers, accountants, lawyers, valuers, builders, etc. Basically, anyone could be a part of this group as long as they know that you buy properties. You see, that is the key, you need to convey the idea clearly: I AM A PROFESSIONAL PROPERTY INVESTOR. Once they understand what you do, you then have to gain their trust. I can't stress enough how important it is for you to act in a professional manner at all times and be true to your word especially in a small country like NZ. You spend a lifetime working on your reputation and it only takes one bad decision for it to come tumbling down. Taking care of these relationships is essential and they take time to grow into meaningful ones. You can't expect to have people offering you off-the-market deals until you become the person they would rather do business with. You need to be the first person they call when they see a good deal available in the market. Not the second person, but the first. I believe that creating a good relationship is all about climbing this ladder until you become number one.

We encourage all our clients to build these relationships and keep nourishing them throughout their investment journey. Take them regularly out to coffee, lunch or just drop in for a quick visit. Learn to listen to them, and I mean listen, not just waiting for time to speak. Listening and asking better questions are the best skills you can work on to establish better relationships. People's favourite topic is always to talk about themselves so let them do so. Creating strategic relationships is all about feeling comfortable with someone and opening up to them. You will never be more open than when you are in the company of someone you feel comfortable with and that genuinely cares about you and what you have to say.

To summarise, here are a few guidelines on creating strategic relationships:

1. Listen.

2. Ask better questions.

3. Be there. Not just once, but on a regular basis. The more you connect the stronger the relationship.

4.   Clearly state what you look for in a property.

5.   Under-promise and over-deliver.

V. **Benefits of Real Estate Investing**

For the few of you out there that still need convincing I wanted to provide you with a quick summary of the top 7 reasons why you should invest in real estate today:

1. Capital appreciation: Real estate can be a great long-term investment, as property values tend to appreciate over time. This means that if you hold on to a property for a long enough time, its value will likely increase, potentially providing a substantial return on investment. This is made even sweeter because of the leverage that banks will provide you with when investing in real estate professionally.

2. Monthly cash flow: When you rent out your property, you can receive a steady stream of income every month in the form of rent. This can provide a great source of passive income and can potentially outpace inflation over time. I have pushed cashflow property for years because I

know that shit happens. When shit hits the fan cashflow property will keep you safe while negative cashflow property will bankrupt you.

3. Diversification: Real estate investing can help diversify your investment portfolio, which can reduce your overall investment risk. By spreading your investments across different asset classes, you can protect your portfolio in the event of market downturns in one specific area. Property has been widely considered to be the safest of all investments and even banks make this very clear by lending at higher rates than in any other asset class.

4. Tangible assets: Real estate is a tangible asset that you can physically touch and see, which can provide a sense of security compared to more abstract investments like stocks and bonds. Bricks and mortar beats spreadsheets.

5. Tax benefits: Real estate investing offers a variety of tax benefits, including deductions for mortgage interest, depreciation, and property-related expenses. These deductions can significantly reduce your tax bill, making real estate investing a tax-friendly investment option.

6. Control: With real estate, you have more control over your investment compared to more passive investments like stocks. You can make changes

to the property, choose the tenants, and decide on the rent rate, giving you more control over your investment.

7. Optionality: Real estate can be used for multiple purposes, such as residential, commercial or industrial. This versatility gives you a lot of flexibility in how you use and monetize your property, making it a versatile investment option. Additionally, real estate can also provide additional benefits like being able to use it as a vacation home or rental property.

Part II – Strategies

I. Fast Property Accumulation Strategy

This is a strategy that has the potential to accelerate your portfolio size and take it to a whole new level. When I finally understood it I was shocked by its simplicity and the amazing results it offered. It targets the quintessential problem of running out of deposit money by recycling your deposits quickly and effectively. In a classic buy and hold investment you will need around six months to be able to refinance your property to be able to take your deposit back out of the deal. Six months is way too long for most investors, but what if you could do it within weeks? Then your investment portfolio could grow to amazing new heights, and this strategy will do just that for you. As I said before, its simplicity will stun you, and its effectiveness will impress you.

Strategies

Applying this strategy is definitely anything but complicated. First of all you will need to find a good discounted deal, preferably with some cosmetic renovations needed. Simple but difficult. Most investors do not know the values in their target area (usually because they don't even have a target area). Then you will do "some" cosmetic renovations. Please read this next sentence carefully. Now you will go to the bank or broker and will explain to them that you have renovated the property and that the value has dramatically increased since you bought it. Get a valuation through one of the valuers approved by the bank and get a new mortgage based on the new valuation price. If you bought the property at a real discount you can take out more than 100% of your deposit and will be able to repeat this strategy as many times as you want. I know that it sounds too simple, and it really is. You just need that initial lump of cash and you are ready to build your property portfolio in record time. The only issue with this strategy is that even after creating a fair bit of equity you may run out of servicing ability, so make sure your portfolio is producing enough cash flow to keep the lending lines open.

Think about it, your portfolio will never be the same again! Now you can accelerate your way to wealth with this new exciting strategy. I can hear some of you thinking: "Yeah, but where do I find those properties?" Well, the answer is simple, become an expert and work hard. Stop making excuses and start making some money. What are you waiting for? Are you expecting it to fall from the sky and onto your lap? There is a Chinese saying that goes like this (you need to read it out loud to get it): Man wait long time with open mouth for roast duck to fly in. The moral of this fun saying is that you have to go out there and make it happen because it won't just happen to you out of divine intervention. The hardest things to do are usually the most rewarding. If the numbers work, go for it and get started accumulating a great portfolio in record time.

So the objectives to this strategy are simple yet powerful. This strategy can help you build your buy and hold portfolio in record time while minimising your risks. Think about it, you can increase your cash flow, replace your income, get the freedom and time that you deserve. But the best thing about it is that with the Fast Property Accumulation Strategy you can accomplish those goals in record time.

One of our clients used this strategy after being taught by my friend, Matt Thorburn, to purchase an outstanding $4 million portfolio within three years. Not only did he use this strategy when purchasing his properties, but he also had a very unique and special criterion added on: <u>All his properties needed to have development potential.</u>

This meant that ALL his properties had to:

Be bought at a minimum of 10% under the market value

Be cash flow positive (8%+ yield)

Be able to produce at least 20% within three months so he could recycle his deposit

Have the potential to further develop (add a minor dwelling unit, subdivide, rezone, etc.).

Now you know why this strategy is so exciting. The potential is huge, especially when you find the right deals with a good amount of equity and enough cash flow to keep the serviceability intact. The sky is the limit, so go get it.

II. Quick Flip Strategy

This strategy is fantastic in NZ especially with its lenient tax system, and you can use it with a mixture of the other strategies to make it even more profitable for you.

Get the process right or you could be in trouble…

To buy a property using this strategy means maybe doing a bit of quick redecorating and then selling it as fast as you can. I said that it works great in NZ because of this reason: there is no capital gains tax here! Well, to be completely accurate you could say that the capital gains tax rate is set at 0%, and you may not pay any taxes if you buy and sell your property and make a profit in the process. This combined with an emerging market like the one we have, makes this strategy almost foolproof.

The hardest part of making this strategy work is finding the right property. I will explain a couple of techniques that I have used to find these great deals. Remember that you do not want to buy property at market price; you want to pick up the great deals and the only way to achieve this is when you deal with a motivated seller. It is very easy to identify a motivated seller. They always listen carefully, they seem anxious about the deal, and they will be receptive to new ideas.

Finding good deals

Usually the best deals are the ones that are not for sale yet. When they go into the estate agent's books it is probably too late.

I really like estate agents; they work really well for me because I know how they think and they know what I want. I am very specific in my requirements, my time is very precious and I hate wasting any of it in pointless viewings of properties that do not match my criteria. Be clear and concise with them or they will even try to sell you their old car.... Seriously, one agent tried to sell me their one-year old Mercedes SL500 because they could not afford to keep making repayments and it was about to be repossessed. Also know that they work for the seller not for the buyer because the seller is paying them, not you. Understanding this simple concept will save you plenty of headaches and misunderstandings in your dealings with agents. The more you work with them and the better the relationship you create with them, the more likely they are to bend over backwards to help you. The hardest part of this game is getting started, once you get going the good deals will come to you regularly without much effort at all.

III. Structural & Complex Renovations

This is one of the strategies I have used the most to make large sums of money over the last two years. This is definitely not for the fainthearted. The problems, delays and big issues that will for sure arise during these deals will test even the best investor. I focused on leaky houses that essentially needed on average 80% timber replacement making them basically a new build. Auckland City Council inefficiencies have made these deals non-viable and I no longer pursue this strategy. When looking at applying structural renovations as a strategy you have to make sure that your current local council is functioning well to make sure they do not cause you costly delays that could easily erode most of your profit margin.

When and if you apply this strategy, you must have a fantastic power team that is ready to go the extra mile for you at the drop of a hat. If you do not have this in place you are crazy to get into structural renovations. You will need: draughtsmen, architects, engineers, builders, electricians, plumbers, drainlayers, plasterers, tilers, painters, etc., and you will need to be prepared to run them or to have a highly paid project manager that will run them on your behalf.

There is plenty of money to be made with larger deals, but never lose track of your actual annualised return on investment. Yes, you could easily make six figures on these deals, but if they take 9-12 months and you have a large outlay of cash your annualised return on investment could just be about 5% and that is obviously not nearly high enough to undertake an activity with such large downfalls. I never touched any deals that did not have at least an expected 30% annualised return on investment and I believe this is the bare minimum to cover you when things go wrong. Understanding structural renovations and their complications could fill a whole new book and to be perfectly honest I seriously doubt many of the readers will ever even attempt to tackle one of them. We do cover some of the best sub-strategies in our mentorships.

These are the top 4 pitfalls while renovating:

1. Underestimating the cost: One of the biggest pitfalls of renovating property is underestimating the cost. It's important to be realistic about the budget, taking into account all the expenses involved, including materials, labor, permits, and any unexpected costs that may arise.

2. Overreaching with the renovation: Another pitfall is attempting to do too much with the renovation. It's important to stay within your budget and not get carried away with overly ambitious plans. Focus on the most important changes and upgrades that will have the biggest impact.

3. Not getting the right permits: Not obtaining the necessary permits and approvals can lead to delays, increased costs, and even legal consequences. Before starting any renovation work, make sure to research the local building codes and regulations and get the proper permits and approvals.

4. Hiring the wrong contractor: Hiring the wrong contractor can result in subpar work, missed deadlines, and increased costs. It's important to do your research and choose a contractor who has a good reputation, is properly licensed, and has experience with the type of renovation you're planning. Make sure to get references and check their portfolio before making a decision.

IV. Contemporaneous or Double Settlements

This is a great no-money-down strategy, but beware it can sometimes get you into trouble when applied incorrectly. I have met several investors who have lost tens of thousands of dollars by taking unnecessary risks. In a sentence, contemporaneous settlement is a property transaction in which you buy and sell a property in one day. If you apply this strategy correctly you will not need to get a mortgage and you will be able to profit handsomely from it.

As opposed to assigning property where you only sell the contract, in a contemporaneous settlement you buy and sell the property in what could be classified as a simultaneous double transaction. You will still be using none of your own money if structured correctly. As a side note, you now have to be a licensed real estate agent in order to be able to assign sales and purchase agreements for a profit. If you are not, then you could be liable to pay hefty fines if you are found out. The Real Estate Institute is currently pursuing anyone who undertakes this type of activity and will take every case they find to court.

Get a good solicitor on board to close these kinds of deals. They will be worth their weight in gold. You will also need a good mortgage broker with good connections with several underwriters.

Let's get started by letting you know what you should do before we get into what you should not do. The first thing you must work on is a good network of buyers (usually investors). These investors will be essential to your strategy since they will become the final purchaser of "your deal". Essentially they are the retail buyer and you are the shop where they get their product which in this situation happens to be a house. At the end of the day what you are doing is finding a "very good" deal and offering another investor a "good" deal so that you keep the "very" part of the deal in profit.

This means that in a good contemporaneous settlement deal there should be enough for each of the three parties that will be involved: the seller, yourself, the first investor, and the final party or second investor buyer. A win-win-win deal.

The proper way of making this deal work is as follows:

Firstly, you sign a sales and purchase agreement in which you will ideally have a get-out clause (due diligence type of clause). Then you will approach your network of investors to offer them an exciting deal. After that you will go unconditional and pay the deposit to the seller, at the same time you should receive at least the same deposit from the retail investor. This way you will cover yourself and will know that the retail investor is serious about the deal.

The next and last step of the deal is that you will end up double settling it on the same day. So the money comes from the second investor's account into yours and then flows into the seller's account (in reality it never actually hits your account). Obviously there should be a substantial difference between what you pay for the property and what the retail investor pays for the property. I would never go into a contemporaneous settlement deal unless I had over $20,000 worth of profit.

There are several potential issues when you try to apply this strategy. You may encounter resistance from some solicitors and mortgage brokers or lenders. Solicitors find problems in deals for a living, so no surprises there. They are trained to find faults and "potential" problems in any transaction that is presented to them. They are usually highly negative because of their job and education. Learn to deal with them and only deal with creative solicitors who will not drag you down every time you talk to them. You only want solicitors that are open to new ideas as part of your team. You will probably only feel resistance from the seller's solicitors, and your own solicitor could play a pivotal role in tilting the final balance in your favour. Having a creative and hungry-for-success solicitor will solve this problem in most instances. The harder problem usually comes from the lenders or mortgage brokers working for the second or final investor. The issue that they will see is as follows: they are offering a mortgage for a property that the seller (in this case you as the first investor) does not even own. Lenders do not like risk, in fact they dislike risk highly. The best way to get around this problem (it will definitely not happen every time) is to once again rely on your creative and friendly solicitor to come to the rescue and explain to the lender what is going on and guarantee them a win-win final outcome.

I have seen several horror stories. The last one was just around two months ago. A friend of mine offered me a property in Wanganui. It was a big renovation job, I would have needed around $30,000 to bring it up to scratch and the price that the property was offered at did not stack up. Done up the property was worth only around $100,000; he was offering me the deal at $85,000 plus the $30,000 that I had to put in it. This would mean a considerable amount of wasted time without rental revenue and me getting a house for $115,000 that was only worth $100,000. In my books that made no sense and I told him he was wasting my time with a crappy deal. Once I questioned him a bit deeper I found out what was going on. He had already gone unconditional on the deal and only had three more days to settle and he did not have any funds to be able to settle. This meant that he was extremely motivated to offload the deal at any means necessary, even ripping off a friend. Be very wary of so called "friends" since sometimes money seems to be stronger than friendship. Obviously I do not keep in touch with my old friend anymore. I have since heard that he owes a lot of money to several investors and he is getting closer and closer everyday to declaring bankruptcy. He took unnecessary risks; do not follow his lead. He made three fatal mistakes on this deal:

1.   He did not offer a win-win-win solution.

2.   He went unconditional without a buyer.

3.   He destroyed his reputation as an investor by offering a bad deal.

Strategies

Never, ever, ever, ever go unconditional on a deal unless you can afford to buy it. If you can afford to buy it there is no risk for you. I really do not understand why people take unnecessary risks on property investing, they may as well go gamble in a casino, at least they will have more fun and get a couple of free drinks.

This story of the deal in Wanganui happens all over NZ every day, please be wary of these situations. Do not get caught as a second investor, and definitely do not become a first investor unless you can afford to buy.

To recap this strategy, just remember that it is a very useful no-money-down deal which will require four main components:

1.   Good network of investors
2.   Good solicitor
3.   Good mortgage broker
4.   The ability to settle the deal.

If you have these parts covered you can potentially make a lot of money. Also remember that you should have a considerable margin to take on the risk. And I will leave you with a final thought ("a la" Jerry Springer): Always create a win-win-win solution.

V. Private Capital Financing

As an investor you will probably run out of money to finance a deal from time to time. My goal is to tell you of other alternatives that are currently available in today's market to obtain this funding.

A. Mezzanine lending/specialist lending/angel investors

You can turn to private capital from investors for finance. A good broker will let you know exactly what is on offer at the time of your consultation. The problem that you will have with this kind of borrowing is interest rates as they tend to be significantly higher than standard banking rates. But at the end of the day, if the numbers work, do not hesitate to get money from them. After all, 40% of something is better than 100% of nothing.

B. Loans from family and friends

Always try to find cheaper alternatives such as a formal loan from friends and family. This can sound like a bad idea to most of you but read on and let me explain how to structure them so that you can minimise the risks.

Strategies

Firstly and most importantly, you need to let them know that this is a business transaction and that no feelings will be involved. Make them sign a document saying that they acknowledge that this is only a business transaction and that the relationship you have with them will never be brought into it. This point needs to be clear before you even explain to them anything about the deal and it is very important for two reasons:

•   The first one is that they will take you seriously – the uncle who used to change your nappies probably still sees you as a kid and this document will get the respect you need to proceed.

•   The second one is that they will know that they will not be able to ask you to change the deal for love or friendship and trust me this will happen unless you specify it. I just lived through a tough situation where someone very close to me tried to change the terms of our agreement because he became greedy and selfish. It was extremely hard for me to stand my ground and continue my relationship with this person on a personal and business level. So remember business is business and family is family, do not mix them up.

Secondly, you need to write a formal loan agreement (secured or unsecured) where you specify several key points like:

•   The quantity of the amount borrowed.

- The term of the loan.

- The interest rate.

- The quantity and timing of the payments.

- Any early redemption penalties, guarantees, charges on assets, etc.

What's in it for the lender?

Now, why would anyone lend you money for investing? I usually ask this question: how much interest are you obtaining on your savings? Usually they say a very small figure from nothing to about 3%. I then ask them if they would be interested in making about 6% interest on their savings. You can make this rate as big or as small as you want – I am just giving you an example. They should now be interested and you can go on to tell them about the loan agreement. Usually they will still be a bit wary about lending you their savings with no security compared to the one they have in their savings account. You can then offer them a charge on one of your assets. This can be anything from your big screen TV to a second charge (see below) on one of your properties.

Charge or Security

A charge on an asset basically means that if the borrower does not meet the terms of the loan, the lender has the right to take the asset that they have a charge on. Now they should be more at ease with lending you money. As I have already explained, your word is the difference between failure and success in this business or in any business. People will line up to lend you money if they know you are trustworthy.

Second charge

I will explain what a second charge on a property means before I go any further. We all know now what a first charge on a property is because most of us have had a mortgage before. When you get a mortgage the lending institution has the right to take the property if you fail to make the repayments. They are not usually in the property business so they will put it up for sale quickly so that they can get their money back. If the property also has a second charge, once the lending company with the first charge recovers all the money owed, the company or person with the second charge will also be able to recover what they are owed with the remainder of the money obtained from the sale. Some lenders won't let you take a second charge when they hold the first one, so ask your broker about the possibility in your specific case. Most lenders will not want you to have a second charge unless there is a lot of equity on your property. Family and friends will be really happy with such security though. Just remember that you will be responsible for paying all the legal bills associated with adding a charge to the property which can definitely outweigh the benefits unless the loan is a considerable one.

As you will be able to see now, there are great advantages in using this form of financing. It is also a great win-win situation for you and your family member or friend to go into this type of agreement together. You get your finance sorted and they will get more money than they normally would. Just make sure to follow the basic principles that I have explained above or you will regret it.

Future gains

Another way of presenting these deals to friends and family is to offer them a part of the future gains. Depending on your strategy, this will be a lump sum, a part of your cash flow or equity released after a predetermined period of time. The profile of the person that will go for such a way of obtaining interest is very different from the one I explained in detail before. The people that will go for this offer will have a higher risk tolerance and they will usually be well informed on the great benefits of investing in property. I could probably imagine as a possible candidate a well-off uncle who works long hours and does not have enough time to find property himself, but is smart enough to have read property investing books on his lunch breaks.

Strategies

Investment deals vs. partnerships

There is a huge difference between presenting an investment deal like the ones I have just talked about and going into partnership with someone. The difference is called control. I want to be in the driving seat of all my investments. Once you start sharing it, anything can happen. This is a risk I am not willing to take unless I really know the person I will be partnering with and that we have a clear and identical strategy for the future of our investment. Besides this, I always write a tight contract in which most eventualities are covered. Partnerships can overcome serious problems such as lack of funding and lack of time.

C. Peer-to-peer lending/social lending

With social lending platforms launching almost every other week, this opportunity now deserves recognition. I am not an expert on this form of funding so I have paid experts to create a report on social lending that will be available to anyone that joins our program.

D. Credit card low-balance transfers

This is a more complex strategy that I personally used to get started 14 years ago. It involves accumulating good debt (renovations, etc.) and transferring it to a low or even better 0% interest-free credit card. Most people freak out when I mention this strategy so I will avoid "freaking you out" and will only explain it when I see you at one of our next events or when you join our program.

VI. Vendor Finance

When you apply this strategy you will effectively be asking the seller to finance part or the whole purchase of their property. You must be thinking that there is no way any seller would ever do anything like this but I will show you the profile of the seller you will need to target who will do this for you.

Vendor profiles likely to go with a vendor finance deal include the following:

a) The first profile that comes to mind is an older couple that are planning to downsize their five-bedroom home with a big garden for a lovely and cosy bungalow close to their grandchildren. They will not need all the money from the purchase price, but they would love to be able to obtain a higher interest rate than what they currently get in their boring savings account.

b) The second profile could be someone who is tired of the noise and the expensive lifestyle in Auckland and who just wants to sell their flat to buy a house in a regional area. They will not need all the money from the sale of their house to buy a new house, and they will be happy to make some interest on the excess money.

c) The third profile I will tell you about is a retiring property investor who now just wants to live off the interest of their investments. They only need a bit of cash and are happy to get interest on the other part they will be lending the buyer. This retiring investor will be more receptive to the idea of vendor finance than anyone else, since they will know more about the property business.

d) I will even write about a possible fourth scenario. A young businessman tired of the stress he has to cope with decides to travel the world for a couple of years. He has a luxury apartment that he wants to sell and is looking for ways to use this money and have it ready in all the destinations he will be stopping in. What we can offer him is to buy his luxury apartment and send him as much money as he needs when he gets to his destinations and we agree to pay the remainder of the purchase price when he gets back in a couple of years. This solution would work great for him and obviously for us.

People in these situations do not need all of the money up front, sometimes they can even finance the total purchase price. They will in this case have a first charge on the property and they will be acting like a lending institution. Don't be scared of asking for this kind of deal if the profile fits – if you don't ask you won't get. Asking will make you money, so don't be shy.

Balloon and deferred payments

I like to give sellers a couple of ways to close down the purchase of their property. Never more than three because you will confuse them, but at least two so that they know you want to help them and that you want to reach an agreement. This is a great tip for getting deals to work. Find a piece of paper and write this down, and the next property you put an offer on remember to give them between two and three options.

I always try to use balloon payments as a way to structure the loan from the vendor, and I also always ask for deferred payments at the beginning of the loan. I can tell you now that it is rare to get more than three months of deferred payments from a vendor, but every bit helps.

A deferred payment means that you will not pay the loan back for a specified time. A balloon payment is one where you will only make small payments (usually just the interest part of the loan) for a specified period of time and when you reach that milestone you will then repay a big lump sum of the loan back.

As you can see, there are lots of possible scenarios where you can apply this technique and a plethora of ways to make it a win-win deal. I am sure you can now think of one that you let go because you did not think of offering them this great way of purchasing their property. Failure is a lot easier to live with than regret.

VII. Buying-Off Plan Strategy

As an astute investor you can get heavily discounted property if you buy property off-plan. Off-plan means that you purchase the property before it is actually built. Usually you would give a small deposit to reserve your property – you can also just pay for an insurance cover to secure your deposit meaning that you could control a fair amount of real estate with a very small outlay.

Why this strategy?

You are purchasing a property at today's prices that will be finished anytime up to two years away. You do this for several reasons – the most obvious one is that if you know that you are investing in an area with potential for capital growth you will have a property with built-in equity when you complete the deal.

 The second reason is because you could possibly assign or double sell the off-plan property to another purchaser before or on completion date. If you do this you will be making the difference between the price you agreed to buy the property at when you gave your deposit and the price another buyer is prepared to give you.

Property development companies

You can usually get better deals at the end of the financial year, especially through the big names in property development companies. The showroom property is usually also a great deal, because you can purchase it cheaper than the rest, and usually you will even be able to let it out to the promoters for a high rent while they try to sell the rest of the properties in the development.

Strategies

Builder insurance policy

When you go into an off-plan deal make sure that the builder has an insurance policy that will cover the eventuality of him going broke before he finishes the construction of the property. I have heard enough horror stories to make this a must check before you even study the deal.

The right price?

Probably the hardest part of buying off-plan is not knowing whether the price you will be paying for the property is too high or not. Do not let developers and salespeople convince you that this is the price that they will be worth in x months and that is why you will be paying it. You want to pay today's prices and this is fair for the developer and for you. I use comparable sales of older properties around the area plus a 15% extra for the premium of having a new property.

Let's say that you want to buy a 2 bedroom apartment off-plan; get comparable sales of already built 2 bedroom apartments around the area and make an average of them. Let's say for the sake of the example that the average is $200,000 – a new apartment should be worth around $230,000. You should never pay any more than this price.

Make sure as well that you have your finance ready in case you need to complete on the deal because you cannot find a buyer. I find these kinds of deals quite easy to do, and very hassle free. If you evaluate the market and the property price correctly, you will make a good and relatively easy profit. These are highly speculative deals and I would only use this strategy at the initial stages of a market cycle. If you use this strategy at the end of the cycle you could end up overpaying for an underperforming property. I saw plenty of people lose everything they owned in 2008 because of these deals.

BUYER BEWARE. Most educational companies out there promoting events and selling their programs are just glorified real estate agents selling crappy new builds from their developer mates for an exorbitant amount of money. Don't get me wrong, I have made a lot of money out of buying and selling new builds but there is a time and a place to do so and these unscrupulous "educators" only care about their profits and manipulate facts and data to bamboozle people into buying properties that are just not good for them.

VII. Lease Option Strategy

These kinds of transactions are very common in the commercial property market and are starting to be used for the residential market in NZ. In other more advanced residential markets, lease options make up a large number of all property transactions.

How it works

A lease option has two separate parts: an option to buy and a letting agreement to the person with the option to buy. The person with an option to buy has the right (not the obligation) to purchase that property for a predetermined time at a predetermined price. In order for this contract to be legitimate and legally binding there needs to be a payment (could be money or valuables) which is very important in the scenario I am about to explain.

You want to buy properties but have very little or no money to get started. You just found a property that definitely needs some cosmetic updating and this is reflected in the under market value price that you are able to buy the property for. You can then offer the seller the following:

Real Estate Mastery

You will purchase the property within four months and in this time you will pay for all the repairs needed to leave the property in a condition suitable for tenants. Then you will explain to them that in order for this to be legal you need to fill out an option to buy agreement which states the costs of the repairs and the time and price of the option to buy the property. Then you will explain to them all the possible outcomes under this agreement so that they will feel safe.

- Firstly and 99% likely, you will do the repairs and buy the property within the specified period of time.

- Secondly, you do the repairs and don't buy the house, in which case they now have a renovated property they can put back on the market at a higher price.

- Thirdly, they decide they don't want to sell the property to you within the agreed period at the agreed price in which case, if this happens, you will have a clause in your option to buy agreement that states that they have to reimburse you with all the projected cost of the repairs, plus a hefty fee for time wasting (make this amount big because your time is worth a lot of money).

Strategies

This is very similar to pushing back the completion day, but this strategy gives us even more time to do repairs, to obtain the right finance and to get the right tenant. Once you have the keys to the property, everything does become much easier and smoother.

Remember that people will be a bit wary of these kinds of deals because they won't be very familiar with them. You have to make them feel at ease. Having a good solicitor in your team whom the sellers can call to alleviate any doubts they may have and to confirm that the deal is legitimate is essential in practice.

Other ways to utilise option-to-buy agreements

The above is quite a simplistic way of using an option-to-buy agreement in the short term. You can use them to do other kinds of medium to long-term deals like the one I will describe now.

You may be tired of having to deal with tenants, or just simply cannot find tenants because you chose the wrong market to invest in (obviously you didn't invest in yourself before investing in property) and you just want out of the property game. At this stage you are looking for a buyer quite desperately. You also know that your property is just a little out of reach for the average first-time buyer, but you know that it is the kind of property that will appeal to them. You can then publish any of the following classified ads to jumpstart some interest.

"Tired of renting? We can help you get your own dream home without having to pay a deposit. Call Anne at 555 1234."

Or

"Fantastic 3 bedroom property in blah blah area for sale. Will suit first-time buyer since you will not need a deposit to get it. We are property investors who can make your dream come true. Call Jo at 543 4564."

You can also place a listing in Trade Me with a title reading: "No deposit or mortgage needed to buy NOW".

After placing any of these two ads you will have lots of people calling to see how they can finally jump onto the property ladder and this will be your chance to explain to them how you can help them. You offer them an option to buy the property within x years at a specific price; the price that you establish will be based on what you think the property will be worth at the end of the predetermined option to purchase. You can play with the amount of time you give the buyer so that it suits your strategy and hopefully their needs.

Strategies

They can move in right away into their new home and pay you the equivalent of what they would be paying for rent in a similar place, plus a top up which is entirely negotiable and will be destined to pay for the deposit of the house when they decide to take the option to purchase. There will be a clause prohibiting them from subletting the property.

You will also require an initial deposit equivalent to roughly 1-3% of the purchase price so that the option to buy is legally binding. Remember that this payment is not a rental deposit; it is part of the payment for the purchase of the house if they exercise the option agreement. You will clarify as well that all maintenance of the property will be their responsibility and if they leave the property, fail to make payments, or decide not to take the option to buy within the specified period, they will lose all the money that would have been destined for the purchase.

Let me give you some numbers so that this concept will be a little clearer:

Property market value today: $100,000

Rental value today: $500

Option to buy in 4 years at: $120,000

Rent monthly: $500

Top up monthly:	$200
Initial deposit:	$2,500

If you play with these numbers you will come up with the payment that the "buyer" has made towards the purchase of the house in the four years that they are tenant-buyers. This payment comes to $9,600 on monthly top ups plus $2,500 up front which comes to a total of 12,100. This means they would have saved up over 10% of their deposit and they would still owe us $107,900 if they wanted to take advantage of this option. First-time buyers will be ecstatic when you show them these kinds of numbers. They need to be pushed to save for the deposit, and this is a great way of doing so.

Once you agree on the terms, you will have a tenant who is not really a tenant; they are a buyer that will take care of your house as if they had already bought it. You will not have to bother with letting agents because they will be taking care of the little inconveniences that will eventually appear in their new house. Statistically only two out of five "buyers" will actually buy the property; break ups, work changes and other eventualities will make up the reasons why tenants will just be happy to lose the money they were effectively putting away to buy their home.

So what do you do when they leave us again with the property if they do not exercise the option to buy? Well, that is your call. You have again several possibilities: renting it, selling it, let it again with an option to buy etc.

If you are looking for great buy-to-let returns, you will usually find them at the higher risk end of the scale with the kind of tenants who rent in the worst city areas. Utilising this strategy can get you great returns, in good properties, with great tenants. I said great tenants because these kinds of tenants have a tendency to stay in a property for a long time.

IX. Reversionary Deals

This very little known strategy has made countless property investor millionaires. It is a common strategy in the UK, and the US. There are only a few people doing it in NZ meaning there is still a huge gap in the market for you to benefit greatly from it. The main purpose of this strategy is to create large amounts of equity in your portfolio. It is definitely not a short-term or cash flow strategy, although you could see massive returns even within a few months. You should only apply it once you build a large amount of cash flow in your portfolio.

The beauty of this strategy is that you can use it to buy property investments as a complete deal (you get the house and the tenant in one strike). You'll now be able to buy superb houses, flats and bungalows, at around half price. Not only that, but they're already fully furnished, completely fitted out and tenanted. And you'll never need to find another tenant! I am sure that you must be very excited by now. The best thing about this strategy is its simplicity and the fact that you actually are helping out people in need.

Many of them come with pre-arranged mortgages so, if you want, you can buy them with low monthly payments out of your income. Please check with your mortgage broker to see which providers are offering mortgages on these deals. They will more than likely be specialist lenders, banks will not usually even know that this kind of deal exists. Having a good broker in your team is once again a major benefit, while having an average broker will definitely slow you down.

Even if property prices never increase again, you'll make over 100% profit in capital growth. This little-known investment strategy virtually guarantees you'll make effortless profits during good or bad economic times while helping people. You will not need any management or estate agents and your own input in time and energy is absolutely minimal.

Strategies

So, exactly what are 'RPIs'? RPIs are real estate transactions in which you will purchase a property at an agreed large discount to let the person you purchase it from live in it (rent it) for a pre-agreed term. The rental you will usually charge in these deals is what is called a peppercorn payment, meaning that you will not actually be charging a rental. So essentially you sacrifice rental income for a large sum of equity to be released at a later date.

How does it fit into my strategy?

RPIs are not for everyone. They are part of a healthy portfolio as a medium to long-term strategy. You should only purchase and RPI when you have enough cash flow from other properties to support the mortgage that you will most likely acquire to purchase the deal. As you can probably tell by now, they are an outstanding way of getting equity instantly and profiting from property with a minimal outlay. Add the bonus that you are helping people out to live in their home until they physically have to leave and you have the makings of a fantastic win-win strategy.

If you want to create a lot of equity quickly into your portfolio, reversionary deals are right for you. They will make you very rich although you will not know when this will happen. You should look at these deals as long-term deals. They are very money hungry, so before you apply it make sure you have other cash flow producing properties to take care of the repayments of the mortgage you will acquire to purchase your reversionary deal.

X. Short Term Rentals

In New Zealand, the rules regarding subletting houses to rent through Airbnb or other short-term rental platforms can vary depending on the specific location and the type of property.

In general, it is legal to rent out your own property on a short-term basis in New Zealand, but there are some restrictions and regulations that must be followed.

If you own a house or apartment, you can generally rent it out as a short-term rental without any specific permission or licenses, as long as it is your primary residence. However, if you want to rent out a secondary or investment property, you will need to comply with the Residential Tenancies Act 1986.

Strategies

If you live in an apartment or townhouse, you may be subject to the rules of your body corporate or homeowners association. These rules will vary depending on the specific development and can include restrictions on the number of nights that a property can be rented out, as well as requirements for insurance and safety inspections.

It is important to also check local council regulations and bylaws, as some councils have implemented regulations for short-term rentals, including a requirement for a permit or registration.

It's also important to note that in New Zealand, you will be responsible for collecting and paying taxes on any income you earn through short-term rentals.

In summary, while it is legal to rent out your property on a short-term basis in New Zealand, there are certain rules and regulations that must be followed, including laws and regulations related to residential tenancies, body corporate rules, and council bylaws. It is essential to check with local authorities and comply with any local laws before renting out your property.

As a tenant in New Zealand, whether you are able to sublet your property on Airbnb or other short-term rental platforms will depend on the terms of your lease agreement and the laws in your specific area.

It is important to check the terms of your lease agreement, as most lease agreements prohibit subletting without the landlord's prior written consent. If you want to sublet your property on Airbnb, you will need to get permission from your landlord.

Even if you have permission from your landlord to sublet the property, it is important to check with the local council and comply with any bylaws and regulations that may apply to short-term rentals in your area.

It's also important to keep in mind that as a tenant, you are responsible for ensuring that the property is kept in good condition and that the lease terms are upheld. This includes ensuring that the property is safe and secure for guests and not causing any disturbance or damage to other tenants in the building or neighborhood.

It's also important to note that as a tenant, you may be responsible for collecting and paying taxes on any income you earn through short-term rentals.

In summary, as a tenant in New Zealand, you may be able to sublet your property on Airbnb, but you will need to get permission from your landlord and comply with any local laws and regulations. It is essential to check with your landlord and local authorities before renting out your property.

Strategies

If you are a tenant in New Zealand and want to sublet your property on Airbnb or other short-term rental platforms, you will typically need to get your landlord's permission in the form of a written document.

One document that is commonly used for this purpose is a "Subletting Agreement" or "Consent to Sublet" that outlines the specific terms and conditions of the subletting arrangement. This document should be signed by both you and your landlord, and a copy should be kept on file by both parties.

The document should specify the terms of the subletting, including the duration of the sublet, the rent to be paid, and any restrictions on the use of the property. It should also include details about the responsibilities of both the tenant and the landlord in regards to maintenance, insurance, and any other conditions.

A good Subletting Agreement should include the following information:

The names and addresses of the landlord and the tenant

The address of the property being sublet

The date the agreement is made

The date the subletting will begin and end

The rent to be paid by the subtenant

The terms of the subletting, including any restrictions on the use of the property

The responsibilities of both the tenant and the landlord in regards to maintenance, insurance, and any other conditions

A statement indicating that the tenant will comply with local regulations and laws, and that the landlord will not be held responsible for any actions of the tenant or the guests

The signatures of the landlord and the tenant

Again, it's important to consult with a legal professional to make sure that your Subletting Agreement is legally binding and complies with all the local laws and regulations.

Create an account on Airbnb.com: Go to the website and sign up for a new account. You will be asked to provide your personal information, such as your name and email address, as well as create a password. Once you have created your account, you will need to verify your identity by providing a government-issued ID or passport.

Strategies

List your property: Once your account is set up and verified, you can start creating a listing for your property. You will be asked to provide details such as the location of your property, the number of bedrooms and bathrooms, and any amenities that you would like to highlight. You will also be asked to set a price for your rental.

Take high-quality photos: Good quality photos are essential for attracting potential renters. Take a variety of photos, including pictures of each room, the exterior of the property, any common areas and local amenities. Make sure the photos are well-lit, in focus, and visually appealing. I can't stress enough how important this is.

Set a price: When setting a price for your rental, take into account factors such as location and time of year. Research the going rate for similar properties in your area and adjust your price accordingly. You should also consider any additional costs, such as cleaning fees and security deposits.

Respond to inquiries: Once your listing is live, potential renters will start inquiring about your property. Be sure to respond to any inquiries or booking requests in a timely manner. This will help build trust with potential renters and increase your chances of making a booking.

Coordinate check-in and check-out: Once a booking is confirmed, coordinate with the renters to arrange check-in and check-out times. Provide them with clear instructions on how to access the property and any additional information they may need.

Keep your calendar up-to-date: Make sure to keep your calendar up-to-date to avoid double-bookings. Airbnb will automatically block off dates that have been booked, but it's a good idea to double-check and make sure there are no errors.

Keep your listing updated: Keep your listing updated with accurate information and respond to any reviews or feedback. This will help ensure that your listing is accurate and that you are providing a good experience for your renters.

It's important to mention that you should check local laws and regulations regarding short-term rentals, so you should be aware of the rules and make sure your property is in compliance with these laws.

Also, as a host, you should aim to create a positive experience for your guests by being responsive, providing extra amenities, providing detailed information, and keeping your space clean and tidy.

My biggest tip as a short term rental investor is to produce and market an experience for your customers. For example, in one of my rentals I have setup and beautiful double outdoor bath house that is a marketing goldmine. The picture of the balinese inspired area just sells the place and means I can charge a premium and get higher quality customers. This specific property would normally get around $20,000 per annum in traditional rent but I get over $40,000 per annum after all my extra costs letting it out in short term basis.

XI. Negotiating Real Estate Deals

Negotiating is all about the art of striking a deal that works for everyone involved. It's the process of connecting with people, exchanging ideas and information, and finding a mutually acceptable solution.

The real estate game is no exception. Whether you're working with your business partner, buyer, seller, agent, or anyone else, the goal is to meet everyone's needs and make things happen the way you want. But, remember that negotiations are not just about the property, they're about people. And, people come with their own goals and interests, so be aware that even the person across the table isn't always on your side.

To ace your negotiations, you've got to know what you want, what the other side wants, and how to use your information, time, and power/authority to affect behavior. That way, you can meet your needs and make sure everyone involved feels like they got a good deal.

When negotiating real estate, it's crucial to adopt your own style. Some folks prefer a competitive approach, using leverage and competition to gain advantage. Others prefer a cooperative approach, using problem solving and creative thinking to reach a mutually beneficial outcome.

Remember, the ultimate goal of real estate negotiation is to profit from the deal in one way or another - whether it's through money, knowledge, or satisfaction. And, it's important to make sure everyone involved feels good about the outcome or at least saves face.

So, go ahead and negotiate like a boss! Just don't take it personally and always keep in mind that negotiations are a business.

Win-Win Negotiations

Okay folks, let's talk about win-win negotiations! It's all about finding common ground and making sure everyone walks away happy. To do this, you gotta get to know the other party's needs and figure out a solution that meets both of your interests. But first things first, you gotta build trust and gather information to understand what they're after.

Don't waste time trying to sell apples to orange buyers. You gotta know their wants and needs first! And forget about the argument, negotiations should be a problem-solving exercise. Shift the focus from beating each other to beating the problem, then everyone wins.

When you're negotiating, think about the interests behind the positions. There are both objective interests (tangible things like money and property) and subjective interests (like peace of mind and reputation). Show that you're willing to do business in a fair and open way, and many people will be willing to share their interests with you.

One of the most important skills a negotiator can have is the ability to see the situation from the other side's perspective. Sometimes, you and your counterpart may have different values, but that's the opportunity for a creative concession. And don't get hung up on price, there are non-price issues that you should raise if they're important to you.

The goal should be for both sides to get a good deal. Don't think about what you can get from them, but what you can give them that won't take away from your position. If you try to help the other side understand your needs and theirs, a lot of the "game playing" will disappear. You both have benefits the other desires or you wouldn't be negotiating in the first place.

People will exchange money for two things: good feelings and solutions. Understanding each other's emotions is key, and remember that real needs are rarely what they seem to be. Focusing on interests opens up new areas of value that may not have been obvious at first.

Know the difference between wants and needs, and make sure you figure out yours and theirs. Getting what you want is only half the battle, it's also important how you get it. Negotiating helps ensure that both sides feel like they got a good deal.

When you're figuring out what to negotiate, make sure you know all the issues, both on your side and theirs. Avoid single issue negotiations because someone is going to win and someone is going to lose. Figure out your own interests and why you want them, then figure out their interests. The more you know, the better equipped you are to find a win-win solution.

Gathering Information

Negotiating real estate can be an exciting and challenging process. To make the most of it, you need to be well-informed about the market, your own interests, and the interests of the other party. Understanding the market will help you determine the right price for a property, so you don't overpay or undersell.

To get a better understanding of what people want, you need to gather information both before and during the negotiation process. This will give you the power to make informed decisions and prioritize your interests. You can ask strategic questions to get more information, and it's important to keep in mind that people's priorities may not be the same as yours.

As you gather information, make sure to rank the priorities of each party involved, including pricing, financing, timing, fees, and legal matters. This will help you determine your negotiating range and when it's best to walk away if necessary.

The key to successful real estate negotiations is information gathering. There's no such thing as a bad negotiation, only negotiations in which one party doesn't have enough information. So take the time to gather as much information as you can, and you'll be on your way to a win-win negotiation!

Planning negotiations can be a ton of work, but it's worth it in the end. Preparation is key to making sure you're not caught off guard. Spend 10 hours preparing for every 1 hour of negotiation. Know what you want, visualize the outcome, and have a positive outlook.

Find out as much as you can about the other side. Get intel from people who have worked with them, learn about their interests and priorities, and try to build trust before the formal negotiations. Know what kind of negotiator you are and anticipate the other side's preferred standards.

Buying and selling real estate involves multiple negotiations, not just one, so prepare for each one before you start. Use standards to give you a fair basis for your goals and to make rational decisions.

And remember, quick deals often result in missed details and unhappy endings. Be patient and thorough in your preparation to increase your chances of success.

Becoming a real estate ninja

Hey there real estate ninja! When it comes to making a real estate deal, always keep in mind to verify before you trust. Don't assume anything about the other side, whether it's their affordability, understanding of you, or belief in you. Do your research and gather as much information as possible before making any concessions.

Strategies

Don't fall into the trap of thinking your adversary is more competitive than they actually are. And when faced with a tough negotiator, don't retreat! Instead, be aware and take steps to minimize the impact.

Understand all the constraints around the transaction, like time and competing offers, and have your info organized for easy access. Know your own personality, knowledge, and skills, as well as the other side's. Trust your instincts if you feel they're untrustworthy.

Be aware of your competition and be ready to talk about it. Find out who the decision-maker is and try to negotiate directly with them face-to-face. Keep your goal in mind and have solutions ready for any obstacles that may come up.

Most people don't prepare well for negotiations, so take advantage of that by preparing well yourself. Talk to others with experience, get inside information, and probe quietly and consistently to gather information about the other side's wants, limits, and deadlines. Taking them out of their work environment can make info flow more freely.

When getting information from their junior staff, act as though the info is new and useful. Some people can be uncomfortable lying and may tell the truth, even if it's not in their best interest. Ask them directly what they want, in informal situations when their guard dogs (lawyers, etc.) aren't there.

Once you know their interests, devise options to satisfy them. Suspend judgement and come up with as many ideas as possible, including wild ones. Consider all the deadlines, including the less absolute ones, and rank your interests to avoid trading a valuable one for a less important one.

Prioritize the issues and determine what you really want. Guess the priorities of the other side and view your own position from their perspective. Share some information to get some, but only after you've done your homework. Introduce new ideas early and several times before the formal negotiation to make them more familiar and acceptable.

Remember that your opponent is also researching your weak points, so be prepared. Talk to your friends, hire an expert, and be ready to share controlled information to lower their expectations. To identify the other side's interests, list the points you want them to agree to and ask what might stop them from agreeing.

Okay folks, let's get ready to get the best deal ever! First things first, persistence and patience are key. Patience is what lets you get all the info you need, especially when you're doing your homework. And speaking of homework, you better be doing your research to know exactly what you want, why the other side should be negotiating with you, and what your alternatives are.

Here's a quick checklist to get you started:

1. Know what you want and what you're willing to give up
2. Research your own weaknesses and come up with a defensive plan
3. Write down your goal and tell someone else about it (accountability is key!)
4. Take inventory of what you have that the other side might want
5. Divide your position into what's moveable and what's not
6. Express each objective in a single sentence
7. Set an envelope for each issue with an opening, target, and bottom line

Know your PLAN B

Now, when it comes to the negotiation, it's time to get creative! Establish trust, ask questions, find out what the other side wants and how you can meet their needs, and try to turn the negotiation into a collaboration. And remember, your bottom line is the minimum you'll accept, but it may change once you know more about the deal.

Lastly, always have a trip wire in mind - an agreement that's not perfect but still better than your Plan B. This will give you an early warning that the deal is going south. And that's it folks! Now go out there and make some deals!

Get the edge

Negotiations can be a real mind game. Power dynamics aren't always what they seem, it's all about perception. If you believe you have the upper hand, then you do. On the other hand, if you think the other person holds all the cards, then that's your reality.

Leverage is tricky, it can change on a whim and often depends on how the other person views the situation. Keep in mind, though, that appearances can be deceiving. The key is to have a strong sense of your own perceived power and use it to your advantage. But don't overdo it and make promises you can't keep.

In negotiations, the buyer usually holds more power because their needs are the focus. But, don't underestimate the seller's power, it depends on their urgency to sell and how bad the buyer wants to buy. It's all about finding the sweet spot between those two needs.

Strategies

The best negotiators are prepared, have high expectations, listen patiently, and stick to their values and principles. Information is key to any successful negotiation, so make sure to gather as much as you can before and during the process. And, if you want to come out on top, have a clear goal in mind and be consistent in your position.

Always have a backup plan, and if the other side says they have options, ask good questions to test their claims. Negotiators with more alternatives usually have more leverage, so make sure you have a few walk-away options up your sleeve.

In the end, negotiations are all about finding common ground and making sure both parties walk away happy. So, bring your A-game, stay calm, and let's make a deal!

Establish Trust

Now, let's talk about building trust in real estate transactions. People tend to be wary of others, especially when it comes to big deals like real estate, so it's important to establish a relationship with them from the get-go.

To do this, be yourself and treat the person you're dealing with as if you're gonna see them again. This way, they'll think of you as a person and not just someone coming to ask for something. Also, try to put yourself in their shoes and never offend them, because once it becomes personal, it's unlikely that you'll be able to make a deal.

It's also important to dress appropriately and be aware of the other person's surroundings, which can give you clues to their values and interests. You can then use that info to build rapport.

When it comes to ethics, make sure you don't do anything illegal and always aim to maintain your personal integrity. If you have a good relationship with an agent, they may be able to help you with unethical dealings. But the best way to avoid these issues is to build trust and establish a reputation of trustworthiness.

Always be open and honest, and express your feelings if you have to. This will help build empathy and get the other person to open up as well. And always be a nice person to deal with, because if they like you, they'll want to please you.

When negotiating, strive for the high moral ground and always provide explanations for your "no." And never take advantage of an obvious error made by the other side. People like to spend time with someone who seems genuinely interested in them, so try to make a connection before making a quick deal.

Strategies

In conclusion, successful real estate negotiations are built on trust. Be honest, maintain high ethical standards, and make sure everyone on your team knows what is and is not ethical. And most importantly, be a nice person to deal with, and make sure your agency displays high ethical standards too.

Negotiator Types

Pragmatic negotiators:

They're all about the bottom line and are short on time.

Don't expect small talk, they just want to get down to business.

Stick to the facts and don't beat around the bush. They're not interested in playing games.

They're not afraid to get aggressive and make threats to get what they want.

They're all about winning, so forget about the "win-win" thing.

If you're selling to them, show 'em respect and give 'em straight-up facts. No need to be too friendly.

Extroverted negotiators:

They're all about feeling good and don't want to get bogged down with details.

They make quick, emotional decisions and are easily excitable.

They want to influence others, so be enthusiastic and make them feel like they're making the right choice.

If you're selling to them, be their friend, have a good time and let them do most of the talking.

Amiable negotiators:

They're all about being friendly and they like a warm approach.

They don't like pressure and make slow, deliberate decisions.

They want everyone to be happy and will often give in to avoid conflict.

If you're selling to them, take it slow, build trust and make them feel comfortable.

Analytical negotiators:

They love details and need all the info.

They make slow, careful decisions and love charts and graphs.

Strategies

If you're selling to them, give 'em all the facts and figures and be prepared to answer a lot of questions.

Conscientious negotiators:

They're sticklers for rules and regulations and need everything to be perfect.

They're not very friendly, but they'll make decisions based on lots of detailed information.

If you're selling to them, show 'em the evidence and give 'em time to think.

When it comes to negotiating, the goal is always to find a "win-win" solution. The best way to do that is to separate the people from the problem, focus on their interests and create options where no one loses. And remember, assertive folks make quick decisions, while unassertive ones need time to think.

Part III – Goal Setting

This is the most important chapter in this book. The way you feel about property investing will define how successful you will be as a property investing professional. The best way to approach property investing is with SMART goals. SMART is an acronym which stands for:

S pecific

M easurable

A chievable

R ealistic

T ime controlled.

I will give you an example of not being specific when setting goals. I've heard lots of people say that their goal in property investing is to make a lot of money. That says absolutely nothing to me – what is a lot of money to you? $30,000? $250,000? $10,000,000 per year? Do you want it to be passive income or do you want to always be involved? You should know the answer to all of these questions before you even look at your first property.

When we talk about being measurable we are talking about something that can be accounted and matched against, for example "I want to buy five houses in the next 13 months".

You need to make sure that your goals are realistic and achievable so that you do not panic or get bored. You do not want to make your goals so high that you feel discouraged, or so low that you get bored. Finding this balance will take some time but once you get it right you will always keep increasing the bar and pushing yourself to the next level.

Time controlled is a key concept – if you do not define time boundaries you will get frustrated and quit. You should also set different goals for different time frames; what you want to achieve in the first six months will be very different to what you will want to obtain in five years.

Goal Setting

Remember one thing when you are doing this exercise. People tend to overestimate what they can accomplish in a short time period (up to six months) and they usually underestimate what they can achieve in longer periods. I could go on and on about this topic for ages, but I wouldn't be accomplishing what I set out to when I started writing this book – I wanted this book to be practical and I will stick to my goal.

The best thing for you to do now is to go to a quiet place where you can just clear your head and think about what your goals are and whether you believe you can achieve them through property. Once you have your goals ready, you have to develop a plan. If you fail to plan, you plan to fail. Planning will design the path you will take to achieve the goals you have just set.

This book was intended to give you more options to help you create your pathway to achieving your goals. After having read all these strategies, you will now have a better "toolset" to accomplish your dreams. Your plan will definitely guide you along the way, and you should always try to stick to it. I intentionally wrote "try" because some new paths will open along the way, and maybe these new paths will take you to your goal more quickly or in a more pleasurable way.

Remember as well that you will find obstacles along your anticipated path. It will not be a smooth ride for most of you. Things will come up to distract you, and you will probably have to withstand quite a lot of negativity by some of your peers. Don't get upset when everything around you seems to be slowing you down. You know where and why you want to get there. Yes I said WHY. It is not enough to just set goals; you need to attach passion to them or they will become just dreams. When you attach feelings to your ideas, they become stronger. You actually use more of your brain when you attach feelings to ideas. So when you are in the quiet area that we talked about before trying to write down your goals, know why you want to get there. It is a major part of this process and therefore part of your future success.

Once you know where you are headed and how and why to get there, you will be ready to take the most important step: taking action. I have seen so many investors who have written down everything they want to achieve, how to achieve it, where to achieve it – they have really done their homework, but they still do not buy any property. I call this "analysis paralysis" and it is a symptom far too common in Western society. And I meant what I said when I wrote "symptom". A symptom is usually caused by a disease. The disease in this case is cultural conditioning. We believe that life is about playing everything "safe" –

Goal Setting

even if we now know that what we believed was "safe" is just a lot of rubbish. Life is not about that; life is about growing, achieving, and sharing with others. We need to constantly challenge ourselves to keep living a happy life. The biggest killer of our mature population is retirement. Your brain is a wonderful tool that needs nourishment; you ought to provide that in the way of challenges. You need to get out of your comfort zone and venture into the joy of uncertainty. Here is where the real rewards grow. This is the only reason why there are not that many millionaires. Most people are just too scared to even try to get there.

The main thing that you should take after reading this book is that you must do something different now to change your outcome. Let me tell you something, if you finish reading this book and within the next couple of hours do nothing about it, you have just wasted a lot of valuable time and the money you invested when you purchased it. To get the most of this or any self-help book you must get motion. Motion is necessary because it creates movement and momentum. Even if it is just a small act like getting a new property investor business card, this small act will get you moving in the right direction. Promise yourself that you will apply at least one of the principles taught in this book for the next week every single day. Make a spreadsheet about it now (this can be your first step of the seven-day process), and start filling in what you did on that day. It is amazing that within a few days you will have accomplished more than you thought possible. Put some offers in, meet some agents and follow up on them, analyse areas, get a mentor.... When you create momentum you are unstoppable. It works like starting an exercise programme. Most people hate the first day, they are unfit and they sweat and feel pain in muscles they did not know they even had. They get home and the pain gets even worse. The second and third day in the gym are not any better and they feel discouraged because they do not see any amazing results. The only results they get are soreness and missing out on TV dinners at home. After around one week of starting the exercise programme they start to feel better about themselves, they have more energy and they can see results! Wow! Now this is what I call momentum. You get hooked on the feelings and more importantly the results. The same outcome applies to property investing, you do your first deal and then you see the money and finally realise that you do not ever need to work for anyone else but yourself. You are the master of your destiny, and that feeling is amazing. You also start seeing the money coming into your account. Just imagine adding zeros to your account balance... Then you feel even better.

Goal Setting

Are you excited yet or what! The analogy of working out in the gym is great for another reason. Most people give up their fitness routine after around six to eight weeks. I have myself been guilty of it. The reason for this behaviour is very simple. It is the concept of reaching a plateau. The word plateau comes hand in hand with the concept of a comfort zone. Let me explain to you how it works in the exercise routine example. You have now been exercising religiously for five weeks, the changes in your body are amazing and you feel great. The problem is that in one week you have two birthday parties and you have to drive down for a whole day to attend a business meeting. Your exercising sessions get reduced to nil during that week because you are either too hungover or too tired to go to the gym. The other problem is that your metabolic rate has also increased and you are now hungrier than ever. Within that week you seem to gain your whole gut back and feel absolutely exhausted. And then you tell yourself the same old lie you have told yourself all your life, this does not work. You should be telling yourself this instead: I did not want it enough to make it work. Exercising works, and so does property investing. You just need to make them work.

You will have problems that you will need to overcome in your investing career. Look at them not as colossal mountains but as great opportunities to grow as a person and an investor. Just like the parties and business meetings in your exercising routine, you will suffer from lack of funds and unexpected costs in your investing career. All these problems are solvable and you won't even remember them in a couple of years. The problems that I thought were huge in my humble beginnings are now just dinner table jokes of how silly I was to even consider them problems. Also like the metabolic rate going up or down, you will also have to live with up and down property cycles. Learn the advantages and disadvantages of them and employ strategies that will let you profit in them. Don't swim against the current, go with it.

Most people also plateau for a different motive: boredom. Going back to my exercising metaphor, they keep exercising at the same intensity and using the same routines for months. After a while they see no new results and exercising is not a thrill anymore, it is just the same old boring push-ups and sit-ups. Lack of excitement equals lack of energy. Soon enough you will be so discouraged and unhappy that you will stop your routine altogether. You brain is too smart to keep boring itself to tears.

When investing in property the same principle also applies. You need to keep evolving as an investor or you will lose your passion that is the fuel that finally will get you the success you are after. New strategies, new markets, new property types…. All these new elements will make you feel excited and will keep your motivation levels high and healthy. Your brain will tell you: please give me more of this because I am having fun! Thrill equals action, and soon enough you will get stunning results that will catapult you into even more excitement because you will start playing with more zeros and different property and investment types. It all comes down to one of the main basic human needs: growth. Our minds and bodies are thirsty for growth. Growth is exciting, it pushes us out of our comfort zones and gets us to achieve new goals in our lives. Learning, reading, meditating, teaching, thinking, inventing, writing, etc. All of these activities will help us grow as individuals, healthy individuals.

Property investing is a process that you must learn to enjoy. Maybe not for itself, but for the results it will produce for you. If your why is big enough, you will have the energy and enthusiasm to overcome any hurdles you may encounter. Find those whys and you will be truly unstoppable.

Our identity is an incredibly powerful force that shapes not only how we see ourselves but also how others see us. Our thoughts and beliefs about ourselves can impact everything from our daily actions to our long-term goals and aspirations. It's important to understand the role that identity plays in our lives, and how we can use this to our advantage to achieve the things we want.

The idea that our identity shapes our behavior is not new. In fact, it's a well-established concept in psychology and has been studied for decades. Researchers have found that people tend to behave in ways that are consistent with their self-concept, or the way they see themselves. For example, if someone views themselves as lazy, they are likely to behave in a lazy manner, whereas someone who views themselves as hard-working will likely be more productive and proactive. This is why it's important to be mindful of the self-talk that we engage in and the beliefs we hold about ourselves. If we believe that we are limited or can't achieve something, our thoughts and actions will reflect that belief, making it difficult to make progress and achieve our goals.

On the other hand, if we adopt a positive and empowering identity, we can use this to drive us towards success. By focusing on what we can achieve and taking actions that align with this, we can create a self-fulfilling prophecy that helps us reach our goals. For example, if you want to become wealthy through property investing, it's essential to adopt a mindset that focuses on finding positive cash flow properties and profitable renovation deals. By focusing on what you can achieve and taking action, you are much more likely to find success.

It's also important to understand that our identity is not set in stone and can be changed over time. This is a powerful insight, as it means that we

Goal Setting

have the ability to shape our identity in a way that aligns with our goals and aspirations. For example, if you want to become more confident, you can start by adopting a confident identity and taking actions that align with this. This could involve speaking up more in meetings, trying new things, and pushing yourself out of your comfort zone. Over time, as you continue to behave in a confident manner, your self-concept will start to shift, and you will become more confident as a result.

In conclusion, our identity plays a crucial role in shaping our behavior and determining our outcomes in life. It's important to understand this concept and use it to our advantage by adopting a positive and empowering identity and focusing on what we can achieve. By doing this, we can create a self-fulfilling prophecy that drives us towards success and helps us achieve the things we want in life.

You need to decide.

Decide comes from the Latin word *"decidere"* which literally means to cut off. In your life you are always deciding. You are always cutting off paths that you may have followed. Even when you think that you will put a decision off and sleep on it, you are really making a decision since you decided to cut off the possibility of deciding right now instead of tomorrow.

Life is full of big and small decisions. You need to decide on all of them. Because you have read this fascinating book, now you are presented with a massive decision:

Do you become a successful property investor or do you keep doing whatever it is you do.

This is a classic case of analysis paralysis. People are often too afraid to make a decision and take action because they fear making the wrong choice. But the truth is, you will never know if a decision is right or wrong until you make it and take action. Every decision brings with it the opportunity for growth and learning. Even if a decision leads you down a path that doesn't turn out as you expected, you still gain valuable experience and knowledge that you can apply to future decisions.

Additionally, it is important to understand that there is no such thing as a perfect decision. Every decision carries with it a certain level of risk, but it's up to you to decide whether that risk is worth taking. The key is to weigh the pros and cons of each option, consider your own values and priorities, and then make a decision that aligns with your goals and aspirations.

So, when it comes to deciding whether to become a successful property investor or not, it is essential to do your research, seek out the advice of trusted mentors, and understand what you are getting into. Property investing can be a great way to build wealth and secure your financial future, but it requires dedication, discipline, and a willingness to take calculated risks.

Once you have taken the time to consider your options, it's important to take action. Don't let fear or indecision hold you back. Take the leap, make the decision, and then commit to making it work. Remember, success is not just about making the right decision, it's also about taking action and following through on that decision.

So, are you going to be a can or a can't? The choice is yours. By making the decision to become a successful property investor, you are taking control of your financial future and positioning yourself for long-term success. So, what are you waiting for? Make the decision and take action today!

It is up to you to decide the right path, the path that will take you to your whys and your goals. You already know which one it is. Most people know what to do but they don't do what they know.

My good friend, Kevin Green, loves and constantly uses this 10 word quote by William Johnsen:

"IF IT IS TO BE IT IS UP TO ME."

He always said that these are the ten most powerful two letter words to form a sentence.

Decide to go for it full steam ahead and never look back. Now you have made your decision towards achieving success, whatever it means to you.

Do you want it bad enough? Desire.

The word desire also comes from Latin. It translates to "of the Father", something obviously divine. Regardless of your religion if any, you will understand what it means. Your desires are divine whys. They are the whys that will make a successful life. They are the whys that will fill you with unlimited energy to get the most out of every minute.

Find your desire and you will find the right path to achieving your goals. You will need time to find what your heart truly desires. Meditation will help you get there. Another way of finding your desire is to do some active thinking. I call active thinking the process in which you sit down by yourself and try to find the answer to a question. As soon as you have an idea, you must write it down and eventually you will get the answer you were after. The processes of active thinking and meditation are unpredictable, and the results could come to you in minutes or months.

Goal Setting

Keep working on it because when you finally get there your life will never be the same again.

Napoleon Hill's *Think and Grow Rich* also talks about what desire means. He actually describes it by defining the commonly used phrase "burning desire". He explains where this phrase comes from. The phase comes from an old navy general who was about to take on a bigger-in-numbers adversary. When they arrived at their destination he ordered all his men to burn the ships that they have travelled in. Doing so would prevent them from even having the thought of retreating and defeat. They now knew that to survive they had to beat their enemies, even if they were outnumbered. It goes without saying that they did win the battle. It is amazing that when we give 100% of everything we have and there is no other escape plan, more than likely we will find a way to achieve our goals. This is how the phrase burning desire started: they got the desire to win because they burned their ships. What ships do you need to burn in order to achieve your goals? What comfort zones will you have to let go of to achieve your whys? Take the time to identify them first and secondly to let go of them to reach a better lifestyle.

Do not feel fear about letting go, remember that we are the happiest and we achieve the most amazing results when we grow and we challenge ourselves. No one remembers the time when you did not take action, but you will always commemorate the times when you did what you knew you had to do. It does not matter whether you won or lost, the only thing that matters is that you gave it your best shot and did not let life pass you by.

Adjust your income to fit your lifestyle.

Most people do completely the opposite. They adjust their lifestyle to fit their income that is why they moan about how miserable life is. They take the role of victim instead of victor. It is a much easier role to play since you don't have to do anything, you just let life do unto you. On the other hand, you can play the role of victor. You will see any adversity that life brings you as an opportunity to grow and contribute. You will see challenges as gifts so that you can be the best you can be and make a difference in the world.

Victims moan, victors enjoy. You need to decide in which side of the court you will be playing. If you are still uncertain about what a victim is, let me tell you a short story that will easily clarify it. An older lady just recently won $2 million playing lottery. You would think that she would be over the moon about the event, but instead she was really upset about it. After being asked why she was upset she answered that she felt hard done by. She said that there was another person choosing the same six numbers on the same day and if that person had not played she would have won $4 million instead of $2 million. Hopefully now you can see what I mean by a victim. Probably you know someone close to you who lives life as a victim. Maybe that person is so close to you that they are even reading this same page of this book right now! Probably I am wrong to say that because a victim would already have thought of an excuse not to keep reading this section of the book.

I am not saying that you should always be positive about everything that happens around you as that would just be unhealthy and fake. What I am trying to say is that you can see each individual event that happens around you for what it really is. Just ask yourself this question the next time that you feel hard done by: what else could this mean? Come up with several new positive answers and you will be amazed at how much better you will feel for it. Stress and victim behaviour come as a result of associating a highly negative connotation to an event. When you associate other more positive meanings to it, the event itself seems to lose importance.

Let's do a quick exercise. Can you remember a time when you felt really stressed about something that just seems like a light joke today? I am sure you have hundreds of these experiences. They all happen because of your associations. From now on you have to see events for what they really are, just events. The feelings that you attach to these events will determine how you feel about them.

Let me give you another example of this very important concept. Several religions on Earth actually celebrate death. They associate a feeling of freedom and happiness to the event. They still miss the people that die, but they do not feel sad about it since they know that they have just started another stage, a stage that comes right after death. In most Western countries the feelings associated with death are very different. You are supposed to feel sad, guilty, lonely, depressed, upset, etc. If you don't feel this bad then there must be something wrong with you because it is not culturally correct.

The funny thing about this example is that they both refer to exactly the same event, death. Both cultures have completely different feelings about them though. Which one do you think behaves as a victim and which one as a victor? I will let you decide.

In any investment that you enter you will have to face challenges. They will come from unexpected places and usually whenever you are not ready for them. Start acting as a victor and you will conquer them. Act as a victim and you are sure to never evolve and will live a miserable life.

Goal Setting

Fake it until you make it.

Most people are so scared about property investing that they never get started. Their fear can be smelt miles away by vendors, estate agents and others involved in the property buying process. This is the main reason why you must fake it until you make it. You need to act like a professional so that you are treated like a professional. When you act, behave and ask questions as a professional property investor, you will experience a different level of service and most importantly success.

Professional property investors are not arrogant or ill tempered. Most successful professional property investors that I know are usually even tempered and humbled individuals who always try to create win-win solutions to every scenario.

You do not even need to wear flashy clothes or drive a Porsche. You just need to look the part and wear nice clean clothes. I have seen people wearing dirty and wrinkled t-shirts when meeting up with their solicitors or estate agents. This just shows a complete lack of respect for them and what you do. If you do not care about yourself, how much will you care about others?

Don't ever lie. You will always eventually get caught, and your name is the most important tool that you have in this world. Faking does not mean lying. When you fake something you are just imitating something that you want to be like. When you imitate and behave like successful people do, you get what successful people get. This is why mentoring is such an exciting tool for investors. You can imitate successful property investors so that you achieve the same results.

Do not be afraid to copy what other people do or the systems they implement. If they make them work so can you. If they profit from them so can you. Just emulate their systems and open your bank account to let the money come in.

Always think of your whys.

If in doubt, go back to your reasons why you got started. The answer will then show itself. Most people get so involved in the detail of the process that they lose track of the big picture. The big picture is the compass that will guide you to your destination. Without it you will feel lost all the way to nowhere.

I love the word nowhere. Whenever I see it or listen to it I think NOW / HERE, because you can go nowhere or you can get started NOW HERE. Once again the decision is up to you.

Goal Setting

I will now tell you the statement that changed my life. Hopefully it can do the same for you too. Failure is easier to live with than regret. What do you want your headstone to say after you die? Will it be something like this?

Here lies David Leon.

He had a nice life, family and friends.

And he never had many problems.

Or would you rather have something like this?

Here lies David Leon.

He enjoyed every second of his exciting life.

The people around him will always remember him for his intoxicating energy.

You choose what will appear on yours. Remember this – you never know when your tombstone will be written, so start acting today! Socrates once said: "To move the world, we must first move ourselves". Take action, do all you can while you are here, enjoy every second of the ride and share it with others. Use this little formula and you will be successful not just in property investing but in your life.

Getting started – so what next?

If you are not sure what your next step will be I can give you a couple of tips. The first one is to get out there and start talking to people. Remember that the personal relationships you make will make you wealthy.

Choose the people you spend most of your time with wisely. Make friends that will push you out of your comfort zone. Get a mentor, someone that is where you want to be and that can take you there quicker and in a safer way since they have already been through the problems that you will surely face in your investing career.

Keep investing in yourself. I am extremely proud of this book and I am positive that it will move you in the right direction towards achieving your goals. Keep reading books, attend seminars, and visit websites that can provide you with useful information so that you can keep growing as an investor.

Get educated and join an investor group. This was essential in my career as a property investor. Someone that is where you want to be and that has done the long yards that you will also have to walk. Investor groups and coaching are the best methods to get the results you want in record time. Make sure that you pay handsomely for your education and power team. This way you will ensure that they will really be working for you and you will not feel bad about calling them or visiting them for advice and expertise. I also noticed that when someone helps you out for free, you do not attach any value to the experience and you will barely take any action at all. When you pay for a professional mentoring or coaching service you will take the necessary steps to at least recuperate your investment, and this by itself will create the momentum that we talked about in the last chapter that is essential to get started and to achieve great success in this or any kind of investment. Work with people who will take the time to know you, your goals and reasons to invest in property.

Start making some offers on property. You will be amazed to see just how many great deals there are out there, but you have to start taking some action to find them. Just add a due diligence clause to the standard Auckland Law Society sales and purchase agreement. This way you will always be able to get away from completing on it. Here is a reminder of the one we use:

Due diligence

This agreement is entirely conditional upon the purchaser approving (in the purchasers' sole and unfettered discretion) all matters that the purchaser considers may touch, concern, or affect the property or the commercial viability of the transaction within 21 complete working days after the date of this agreement by both parties. If notice is not received in writing by the vendor's solicitor or agent by 5pm on the 21st complete working day after the date of this agreement of the purchasers' approval of the property, then the contract will be at an end. This condition is inserted for the sole benefit of the purchaser.

Don't be afraid of a small confrontation with agents. I found that most of the agents I did have an argument with early in our relationship have now become the most valuable ones in my power team. I guess that being a straight shooter has its benefits.

And finally, I ask all my clients to write down a personal contract. This contract helps them to get started in the property investing world. Please re-write it and make it happen:

I, [insert your name here] promise to purchase one or more property with the objective of renting it or selling it for profit within the next 90 days.

Date   Signature

Goal Setting

These are simple steps you can follow to keep achieving wealth for the rest of your life. Keep investing in yourself and the rewards will be infinite.

So what are you doing still reading this book? Go out there and get started NOW! Life is too short to waste, start really living today!

About Real Estate Mastery Limited

Real Estate Mastery was co-founded by David Leon to provide people with the resources to get into profitable property investing regardless of their current circumstances. Real Estate Mastery teaches active and passive strategies that will deliver results whether you are a hands off investor or even if you don't have any money to get started just yet. We invite you to have a look at our webpage and watch some of of our videos to see how Real Estate Mastery can assist you to getting better results. www.realestatemastery.co.nz

Testimonials

"A simple yet insightful book that highlights the best strategies available to profit from in real estate. A must read to all investors regardless of experience" Benn Doyle, Award Winning Property Developer and Investor.

"Yet again another great read by David Leon. Practical strategies explained clearly." Kevin Green, BBC Secret Millionaire & one of the UK's largest private landlords.

About the Author, David Leon

David started investing in real estate in England in 2002. He used creative strategies to purchase properties using none of his own money because as he puts it "I didn't have any money anyways!". Over the next few years David applied the same strategies that yielded so handsomely in Spain and New Zealand. The success that he achieved has led him to share his story on stage alongside some of the most accomplished property investors and entrepreneurs in the planet like Sir Richard Branson, Robert Kiyosaki and Grant Cardone. David has invested in several other countries since and created several multimillion dollar property businesses. He is the co-author of the best selling book "Successful Strategies to Build a Fortune in Real Estate" published in 2007 and of "Lazy Happy Successful".

www.ingramcontent.com/pod-product-compliance
Lightning Source LLC
Chambersburg PA
CBHW031856200326
41597CB00012B/442